THE REST OF MY
L   I   F   E

BY LAURA RUSSELL HUNTER WITH POLLY HUNTER MEMHARD

With grateful acknowledgement

"Caleb & the Sow" is reprinted by permission of The
Stephen Greene Press from *The Old Timer Talks Back*
by Allen R. Foley. Copyright © 1975 by Allen R. Foley.

The photograph of Queen Elizabeth on page 33 reprinted by permission of Keystone Press Agency, Ltd.
Copyright © by Keystone Press Agency, Ltd.

The article in the Epilogue, written for this book,
"The Rest of *Our* Lives: A Positive Approach to Aging"
is copyrighted © 1981 by Ken Dychtwald, Ph.D.

THE REST OF MY LIFE
Published in the United States of America by
Growing Pains Press
22 Fifth Street, Stamford, CT 06905.

Library of Congress Catalogue Card Number: 81-85425
ISBN 0-941834-01-8

Copyright © 1981 by Polly Memhard

Dedicated to the Heroes and Heroines of Hopmeadow Home

All the events and conversations herein actually took place. However, the name of the Home has been changed, as well as the names of family, friends and residents of the Home, in order to protect the privacy of all concerned. Only the names of the authors, Laura's husband and namesakes and public figures have been retained.

In Appreciation

To Richard C. Memhard, for a wonderfully sustaining relationship of twenty-seven years;

to Ede Baldridge, whose editorial support and assistance arrived at a critical time;

to Robert E. Moran and Nancy Batlin for the cover and book design;

to the many friends who read, commented and encouraged;

and to the wonderful family from which I came and to which I belong, who shared the love of Laura Russell Hunter.

C O N T E N T S

The Rest of My Life
PREFACE

vi

P R E F A C E

Laura Hunter reached the age of eighty bedridden, arthritic and crotchety.

In the ten years after her husband died, her health and spirits deteriorated dramatically. Relying on drugs, and incapacitated by fears of impending change, illness and death, she clung to her radio for company and turned away even her closest family and friends. She rejected all pleas and efforts by her three children to seek alternative care or move to a place where she would have better attention and more company.

When she was suddenly hospitalized, family and doctors had an opportunity to intervene. The decision was made—with trepidation—to place her in a nursing home.

What followed was totally unexpected!

Recovering from the shock, Laura began regaling the family with stories about her life among the "ancient, infirm, odd people." At her daugher Polly's suggestion, Laura started a journal, which grew into a sensitive, colorful and revealing chronicle of this dauntless woman's life at "Hopmeadow Home."

Polly has shaped the journal into a book and brought it to publication with the hope that moments of "music, love and laughter" from her mother's life would continue to reach others, helping them to relish old age and to have the courage, as Laura did, to transform endings into beginnings.

Husky

SEPTEMBER

ebbing at eighty

There are some days, when you are eighty, arthritic, living alone, and have just had five teeth extracted, (leaving six), when you are tempted to give it all up.

When you were once known as "Husky", shinnied up telephone poles, played the cornet for a Christmas carol sing, ran the Church Women's Group, toured continents, and had friends located all over the United States, Europe, Hawaii, even South Africa,—being stuck to your bed, bathroom and radio doesn't leave much to live for. The children are all about their own lives, and don't really need a grumpy old granny.

That was my thought, anyhow, when I suddenly found myself in a hospital bed, and a new, young doctor says to me:

"Laura, you are not going home."

Imagine, someone who could be my grandson, telling me what I'm going to do for the rest of my life! But he is a very attractive young man, nice enough to be my grandson.

He and my son, Ben, seem to be in cahoots, cooking up plans for my future.

Next thing I know a Mrs. Starr, from Hopmeadow Home, has come to check me out to see if I can dress myself, walk to meals, make my bed and pay the bills. I tell her I am not interested in going anywhere or doing anything, least of all getting up for a seven-thirty breakfast. I haven't been out of bed before nine a.m. for at least ten years, since Payson, my cook and housekeeper, has always brought my breakfast on a tray at eight o'clock.

I have no intention or desire to change anything, or go anywhere, except back home. But I *can* dress myself, as long as I dispense with underpants and zippers up the back.

O C T O B E R

the plunge into Hopmeadow

It is worse than I had imagined. Being put in a rest home, where *everyone* is either elderly or disabled or both, is outrageous. I look around and I ask myself, "*I* belong here, with all these ancient, infirm, odd people?"

It is strange and confusing, with miles and miles of corridor between my room and the dining room. I'm assigned to a table of strangers, who stare without saying a word, while I try to down a sticky, soft-boiled egg without losing my painful, new, lower denture. Sometimes it pops out unannounced, and then I stuff it in my napkin and quickly head back to my room, stopping to catch my breath a few times along the way.

I don't see another soul who is at all youthful, but then I have to concentrate pretty hard on putting one cane in front of the other, to see too much who is here.

I lie on my bed, and I think about leaving a five bedroom, four bathroom house, with attached greenhouse, on three lovely acres. What do I get in exchange? One room, fully carpeted, a high bed, and an adjoining bathroom with a high toilet seat. Bars to hang on to, and buttons to push.

No worries, like the house needing paint, the dishwasher needing replacement, the trees crowding in on the house, the heater breaking down, or Payson going on vacation.

Now someone else worries. I understand his name is Mr. Pfeiffer, the Director of Hopmeadow.

Mr. Pfeiffer came to call on me. He sat on the edge of

2

my bed and yelled, until I finally told him I wasn't deaf! We discovered we are members of the same Congregational Church!

Nor, as it turns out, is everybody a stranger. Clare, an old neighbor, has been here for some time. She now stops by to accompany me to meals, which helps because I might easily lose my way. She can walk faster than I can, but she's here because she forgets things. At least she can remember where the dining room is.

In addition to Clare, I have found an old friend, Mildred Winters, whose husband taught our son math many years ago. Mildred dug into her records and has just produced a Christmas card we mailed them ten years ago, with photos of all our grandchildren (there are two more now).

Mildred is several years my senior—five, I believe. She's a good sport, and seems to have one of the best minds here. She invited me to her room—on the same floor but in another direction—which is chock full with her own desk, a typewriter, and piles and piles of books. She is the Hopmeadow librarian, and writes book reviews for our monthly newsletter. She has been keeping me company these first few weeks, and tucks me in bed with a kiss each night.

The staff seems somewhat concerned about my getting enough protein, since I can't chew meat without my new denture flipping out. So I hear the nurse calling me over the intercom at ten in the morning, and again in the mid-afternoon, to come to the dayroom for an eggnog or glass of prune juice.

This morning I had just got out to the day room, and sat down with my glass of prune juice, when something slipped and there it was, all in my lap.

"DAMN!", I exclaimed, without thinking, much to everyone's shock and Mildred's merriment.

NOVEMBER

encounter with a psychiatrist

Unbeknownst to me a psychiatrist was called to come and visit me. I have no use or need for a psychiatrist, since I'm quite happy staying on my bed all day, listening to my radio, and I get plenty of exercise just struggling to eat three meals a day.

But the nurse announced that Dr. Streif was coming on Sunday afternoon at two-thirty. I had already paid 75¢ for a cocktail, for the first party since I've been here. I waited and waited, and the doctor finally arrived over two hours late. I was so *mad* at him for keeping me from the party that when he arrived I told him I had no need for him and marched out of the room so I'd get to supper on time.

The next day he called my son, Ben, who I guess had helped arrange the visit, and asked, "Why is your mother so hostile?" Ben scolded the doctor, telling him I was mad because he was so late. The doctor said I needed pills. We agreed I didn't need *him*, but we still got a bill!

I must admit, I do occasionally get quite mad at the nurses who constantly want to send my clothes out to the laundry. They tell me that I've spilled down my front and I can't wear the dress again until it's cleaned, but it looks perfectly fine to me. I've even received compliments for being the best-dressed lady in Hopmeadow. I have oodles of clothes. So who cares how old they are?

DECEMBER

emerging faces

The faces of my tablemates are beginning to emerge, along with their names. I thought for sure a man was sitting in the wheelchair on my right. He wears pants,

4

has short, white hair, smokes a cigarette through a black filter, and puts his feet up on the hassock in the lounge after dinner. But today I learned from Mildred his name is Harriet. He (she) is very hard to understand and doesn't ever say much. In fact, no one at my table says much, except Hazel, who sits on my left, and she's hard of hearing, so she's hard to talk *to*. As a result of this our dinners and suppers are pretty tedious affairs.

Breakfast is quite different, because many of the people from the medical unit downstairs stay in their rooms for breakfast. The dining room is half empty, and we're assigned to different tables. The people at my breakfast table are all very bright and good conversationalists. We talk so much we're usually the last ones out of the dining room.

There are three Hunters here, along with a Fox and a Wolfe. Mildred made a joke of it and put it in the newsletter.

There's an especially nice aide, by the name of Julie, who is from England. She has done some of my laundry and mending and helped me a lot. We aren't allowed to tip, so I can't do anything for her, but her daughter just got married, so I gave a nice gift to her daughter. Julie and I talk about the Queen and the Coronation, which we both saw in 1953.

J A N U A R Y

exercise class

My son, Ben, came to see me, and since I'm always in my room, lying on my bed, but wasn't, he couldn't imagine where I was. He asked the nurses to look for me. They searched the lounge and corridors and the walks outside, and finally found me—in exercise class!

It's pretty ridiculous, sitting in a chair, waving arms around, stretching face muscles, wiggling toes. But Katie, who runs the class, is very good. She plays soothing records, and it's quite relaxing. Ben seemed very happy that I had left my room and joined a class of my own volition. I guess it's better than doing nothing.

rush for a snooze

I notice that many people rush through their dinner at night, which is at five o'clock, so they can get back upstairs to the dayroom, and claim one of the eight chairs that form a semicircle in front of the television. By the time I come by, perhaps a half hour later, since I sit and visit with the ladies in the lounge, there they all are— most of them sound asleep, their chins resting on their chests, or their heads tipped back, mouths open, snoring away!

Ann Landers

Something I've begun to do each morning is to stop off in the dayroom on the way up from breakfast, where everyone collects to get their morning pills. Phoebe, who doesn't say very much, but who seems to like me, and blows me kisses every time she sees me, always saves me a nice, big, armchair. She sits in it until I arrive, and then she hops up and makes me sit down, while she goes and pulls up another.

While we sit around waiting for the nurse to come with her cart and dole out pills and put in eye drops, Mildred usually reads Ann Landers to us from the morning paper. There are some pretty wild topics and some days it gets hilarious.

baby pictures

The program director, Meg, has asked each of us to provide her with a baby picture of ourself. I looked through all my old scrapbooks that Ben had brought over and found one dated 1896, when I was one year old. Meg put it up on a display board in the gallery, along with several others, and we are supposed to guess who's who. Soon Meg is going to take pictures of us now, to match up with our baby pictures. It was suggested that she get everyone in the same pose as they were in their baby picture, but in some cases it would be quite difficult, and even somewhat embarassing!

relinquishing the house

We've decided to sell my house, since I really am better off here. I don't have any worries and I get very good care and there's lots to do. It means giving up Payson, after he's been with us twenty-five years, but he already has had an offer from a neighbor, and at much higher pay! Payson and I have never talked much before. He is such a proper English butler, that while he was working for me, his most intimate comments were: "Yes, Madam," and "Dinner is served, Madam", and "The dishwasher is broken, Madam." Now he's telling me all about his health and his fishing and his new employer, and we have lots of laughs.

F E B R U A R Y

politics and laughs

Senator Allen Berkley left money for this nursing home, originally intended for elderly and indigent Con-

Laura Russell, 1896

necticut women. It opened five years ago for anyone over the age of fourteen who is accepted by the admissions committee. There are a few young people here, and many more women than men, unfortunately.

I went to an assembly meeting and the secretary, one of the residents, read the minutes of the last meeting. Then the ninety-five year-old elder of the two Berkeley nieces who live here spoke up from her wheelchair (the first words I've heard her speak):

"Hopmeadow comes from the hops the Indians grew in the meadows." Hops, it seems to me, is used in making liquor. I wonder if that's how Senator Berkley made his money!

The younger of the two nieces is Hannah Strait, age eighty-nine. She's a very proper woman, whose gray hair is done up in a neat bun. She wears rimless glasses and speaks slowly and precisely. She is President of the Council and is very active running things. She's a college graduate, and I am quite scared of her, she is so smart.

One morning when the minister didn't turn up for the regular Thursday morning service, Mrs. Strait took his place. I think she's a very religious woman, and I'm afraid I'm not proper enough for her.

I had a laugh one morning, when it was terrible weather. I passed Hannah on my way to breakfast, and she said:

"Not a very good morning."

I replied, "No, and my son and wife are leaving from Bradley Field for Bermuda at eight; I hope they get off all right!"

"Are they driving?", she asked. I laughed, and told her she must be sleepy. It was fun, being able to laugh at the dignified Mrs. Strait.

dressing gowns

At first I didn't much care what I wore, but I have found that other people do. For breakfast many of the ladies wear dressing gowns. On colder days I wear my long-sleeved blue gown, and on warmer days I wear the lightweight red one. People have begun watching me, using my gown as a weather indicator. They say,

"Oh, it's a warm day today, is it, Laura?"

One morning I was putting on the blue gown and I couldn't find the belt, a long, blue cord. I looked all over the bed, the floor, the bureau (that's all there is in the room), and then I checked back in the john. There, coming out of the toilet, was one end of my belt! I finally retrieved it, with two strong hands and a good deal of tugging.

Downstairs at breakfast, I reported my tug-of-war with the toilet to the other ladies, before "Lindy", the one gentleman at our table, arrived.

the most beautiful girl. . .

I've been talked into using the beauty parlor which is just down the hall, and I go every other Friday for a shampoo and set, and I get a manicure as well, since there isn't much else I can do while I'm sitting.

Today I had a permanent from right after lunch until three o'clock. I went straight back to my room and fell asleep and I just happened to turn over and the clock said five o'clock, so I rushed down the hall toward the elevator to get to supper on time.

Halfway down I realized I had forgotton my lower denture, so I had to go all the way back to my room. That made me late, because I'm pretty slow. When I finally got to the elevator, Muffy, the little lame girl, was just getting on, and she held the door and said to me,

"I'm going to dinner with the most beautiful girl in Hopmeadow."

Before we sold my house, Polly, my daughter, brought me a little brocaded French purse that snaps closed, from my bureau. I didn't even know I had it. It's just exactly the right size to put my change and mailbox key in. I keep marvelling about it, since it's just what I need. I tuck it in a little loop-handled bag, sewn by Evie (her husband was a builder), who makes them in the craft room. I loop it over my finger as I hold on to my cane and walk to dinner. I always stop at the mailbox after dinner, and bring my mail upstairs to read in the afternoon.

"Caleb and the Sow"

Mildred gave me a book on Vermont humor, by Professor Foley of Dartmouth College. When I came to the story "Caleb and the Sow," I laughed out loud all by myself. Next morning I read it to the Ann Landers group after breakfast, and at dinner time I took it to my table, and then gave it to Joyce, the head of the dining room, who enjoyed it and took it to the kitchen, to show to Archie the chef, who came out and told me it made his day!

The story is:

"Caleb was inclined, at times, like some others we know, to take too much to drink. His wife, Mary, labored with him patiently and at long last, after about thirty years, he seemed to have gone over pretty well to the side of abstinence.

Then one night after an encounter with some chronies, Caleb came home no longer sober. Mary, disappointed and angry, finally, said, "You're not to sleep in this house tonight, Caleb Jones. Grab yourself a blanket and go out to the barn." He went.

11

Along about three in the morning Mary roused from her sleep, reached over on her husband's side of the bed, and then suddenly remembered her rough treatment of Caleb. Remorseful that she had kept him out of his own house after thirty years together, she got up, lit the lantern, and went out to find him. Mary expected to find him in the horse barn, but he wasn't there. She tried the cow barn; no Caleb. She couldn't believe he'd bed down with the pigs—but there she found him, sound asleep next to a friendly sow.

Presently he stirred in his sleep, turned toward the old sow and began running his hand along her belly. And, as Mary waited in the corner she heard him mutter, "Mary, old gal, didn't remember you had so many buttons on the front of your nightgown."

a timely installation

My house was sold, and my three children took everything they wanted before selling and throwing out the rest. There isn't enough space in my little room here for much, and I didn't really want anything except a chest of drawers, a little lamp, and some pictures. But at the last minute I thought to call and ask them to bring me the large, circular thermometer from the breezeway next to the garage, so it could be put up outside our Home for the residents to see, since they are always asking me what the temperature is.

I put it out on my little balcony temporarily, and then I spoke to the head maintenance man about putting it up outside the dining room where everyone could see it. But he was quite adamant, saying he couldn't put anything up, that the place would get quite cluttered and it just wasn't permitted. So I decided I'd get support from Hannah Strait, and I told her about it. She quite approved, and she suggested I speak directly to Mr. Pfeiffer on this matter.

So then I invited Mr. Pfeiffer to come to my room and see the thermometer. He came, and yelled at me again, and I reminded him I wasn't deaf. He thought it an excellent idea, and promised to have the thermometer installed outside the dining room window within two weeks.

At two-thirty the same day, when I went out for a walk, it was already in place, and now everyone can see what the temperature is outside as they walk into the dining room.

joining in

There's a Book Review Club which meets weekly, and everyone is asked to tell about some book, so after practicing it in my room, I read to the group "A Way of Life" by Sir William Osler. There were about ten people there and they seemed to like it.

Mildred is teaching Yola English, so she can become a citizen. Yola came with her husband from Lithuania in 1943, escaping from the Russians, and worked in the tobacco fields in Connecticut, here in the valley along the river.

A woman from the Legislature came to give Yola her test, and afterwards we had a party to celebrate her citizenship. Now she'll be able to vote in the presidential elections in November.

Yola knits constantly, and when my son, Jonathan, and his wife, Sara, were here with their two youngest daughters, Yola gave each of the girls a knitted hat.

I have found that I can keep Dubonnet in my room and I like inviting guests in for a drink before our dinner at five o'clock. We use paper cups and Polly brought me the silver tray which my husband received for his twenty-fifth anniversary at Cardinal Life Insurance Company, engraved with all the signatures of his agency managers.

So I asked a few friends to come for a drink, and I told them about the time when I was a senior in High School and the Music Director put on a Christmas carol sing at the Isle of Safety by the old State House on Main Street. He asked me if I would play the cornet, which I'd been doing for years in school performances. The platform was built, the crowd arrived, the Glee Club was there, and bright lights were all around. It was a bitterly cold evening, and I remember looking down on the sea of faces, with people jumping up and down to try to keep warm. But it was *so* cold, no one could sing or play, so the crowd was dismissed and we all went home.

The next morning the paper reported:

"Miss Laura Russell was to have played her cornet—but her valves froze!"

M A R C H

important move

After six months of sitting politely at dinner and supper at a table devoid of conversation, I decided I couldn't stay there for the rest of my life.

My friend, Isabel, arranged for me to sit at her table where a vacancy occurred. Ethel, who suffers from some lung problem, doesn't like the location next to the kitchen door. She claimed there was a draft every time the door opened, and she requested to be moved.

So now I sit in Ethel's place. The morning I moved, I told my daughter, Polly, on the phone: "I'm the luckiest gal in Hopmeadow, because I'm at the table I like, where I can look over the whole dining room and see all my friends, and also look out all the windows and see the lovely trees and foliage outside."

14

Laura Russell, 1915

Lindy, the only man at our table, has to watch his diet because he has diabetes. He has just retired, so instead of getting up at five-thirty every morning he is here all day and wondering what to do with himself.

One thing he does is to watch me at mealtimes to be sure I get enough to eat, and also to tell me if I spill down my front. When that happens, he doesn't say anything, he just points a finger at the spill, and I quickly mop it up.

Isabel decided to go Lindy one better, and with great ceremony presented me with a bib at supper one night. I ask the waitress for it when I come in, or else they have it waiting for me at my place. We giggle a great deal at our table, and sometimes get quite loud. Mildred, who sits at another table, now has a signal for me. When she hears my voice booming through the dining hall, telling a story not intended for all, she raises her hand and waves at me until I see her and pipe down!

on the African trail

Hopmeadow gave a dinner honoring the ministers who come to conduct services every Thursday. Mildred and I were invited to sit at the head table, along with Mr. and Mrs. Pfeiffer.

I sat between Father O'Leary and a Mrs. Jones. I felt I had to make conversation, so I told about reading in the paper a few months back about a couple who had moved to Ashford from South Africa. I enquired if either of them knew of such a couple, since I had friends in South Africa, who had visited us in Ashford, and I wondered if the couple who just came from there might know them. (My friend's father had been Lord Mayor of London). Mrs. Jones volunteered to find out, and the next day she called to say the Chamber of Commerce informed her that a Mr. and Mrs. Osgood, who lived in Brookfield, (not

Ashford) had come from East Africa (not South Africa). I was wrong on two counts!

Nonetheless, I called and talked with Jeanne Osgood, and she was most friendly. Her mother-in-law resides with them and her husband, Frank, is off on safari in Africa for four months.

Jeanne came to visit me and brought a wooden carved letter opener with an African head. I served tea, which Jeanne had to go and pick up from the snack bar. She was once a nurse and a midwife, so she is very understanding about a place like this. We got along very well. Jeanne is just about the age of my daughter, Polly.

visitors and gifts

The people who bought my house came for a visit and they brought me a bunch of daffodils from my front lawn and the jade bell push from my dining room table, all polished and clean, which had been left inadvertently when the house was cleaned out. It had been sent, long ago, from our prestidigitator friend, from Gumps in San Francisco. It is a "hand carved jackwater buffalo oriental bell push, symbolic of spring and architecture, and one of the twelve signs of the Chinese Zodiac." That all came from a card which Polly found in a drawer of a teacart I gave my granddaughter, Judy. My sister, Miriam, is going to take the jade to a jeweler to see about making it into a brooch.

Another delightful surprise happened when I opened my mailbox today—and discovered a check for $2,624.78 from the estate of my second cousin, Eleanor Hatch. I and my two sisters each received that amount. I decided I could afford to call each of them, Florence in Oregon and Miriam at Lake Sunapee in New Hampshire. When they answered, I said, "Hi! This call is on Ellie Hatch!"

After supper I sat with the two Berkley sisters for a half hour, and told them my frozen valve story. Even Mrs. Potter in her wheelchair laughed, and I've never seen her crack a smile before.

A P R I L

developing friendship

Isabel is one of my best friends here. We've found we have been to many of the same places as each other, such as Madeira and Mallorca, where we stayed in the same hotel, even! Her husband was head of a big company and we get along well. I think she must be quite wealthy, because she buys her liquor by the case, and stores it under her bed! She also confided to me she's giving a gift to Hopmeadow of a recreation area (all completely anonymous), and it's costing several thousand dollars, I'm sure.

nominations

I attended another meeting of the Assembly, which includes everyone who lives here, and Mr. Pfeiffer asked for nominations for the Nominating Committee. Someone put my name up! Then we were told to vote for one, closing our eyes, but apparently some people voted more than once, because Mr. Pfeiffer said it wasn't legal, and went out to get some paper for ballots. When all the ballots were counted, I had been elected to the Nominating Committee.

Union Church revisited

A letter has arrived from the current President of the Union Church Women's group, inviting me to attend a

18

party honoring the past presidents. I called my sister, Miriam, who said she'd take me, so I accepted.

I decided to wear the dress I wore in England at the time of the Queen's Coronation, in 1953. Nobody around here has seen it, and it looks as good as new in spite of being twenty-four years old. *(Now '77)*

Miriam picked me up after supper, and when we arrived, there were eighty-five women at the church. I was the oldest person there, and I was presented with a corsage. My chair was too low, so it had to be puffed up with some spare pillows.

A new young organist and a member of the choir entertained.

When I had an opportunity, I told the story of the time when I was President of the group, and I happened to be rather large, being eight months pregnant. This was in 1930. There was a church meeting, and Archibald Austin, then minister of the church, a great, towering man, introduced all the heads of the committees to the congregation. When it came my turn, he looked down at me, and said: "I would like to introduce the President of the Women's Group, in the shape of Laura Hunter!"

Miriam brought me home and I was in bed by ten-thirty. As I think about that evening, it's funny how old so many of that group looked to me. They really were *worn out.*

I forgot to wear the corsage the Churchwomen gave me to two suppers, but I remembered the third evening and I put it on with my light blue suit and print blouse. As I approached the table, Isabel asked quite loudly: "Who's keeping you?"

elections

At the first meeting of the Nominating Committee we went through the list of residents with Mr. Pfeiffer,

19

looking for the best brains to help serve on the Council. We ended up with three of us nominating each other for the Council of eight. There just aren't many people here who can hear, see, talk, and remember what they're doing. A week later, the residents voted us all in!

seed money

At my first Council meeting the Treasurer had little to report, since the Council doesn't have any money. It seemed to me, since we're planning a fair in September, we needed to have some seed money to help get the fair going. So I wrote a letter to Mr. Pfeiffer, and enclosed a check for $100, asking that the gift be kept anonymous. A few days later I received acknowledgement for the check, in which Mr. Preiffer wrote my gift would be kept "anonimous."

Next time I saw him in private, I asked him, "How did you get to be Director, if you don't know how to spell anonymous?"

The fair is planned for September 9. Isabel suggested it, as she was head of a fair at her church which raised several thousand dollars. We voted in assembly to see what to raise the money for: a new auditorium, a swimming pool, or a van with a special elevator so it can carry someone in a wheel chair. I wanted the swimming pool, but the vote went in favor of a new van.

retirement

I made the rounds and called on twenty-six people in my unit, carrying a notebook and pencil in my purse, and I asked each person for ideas about the home and if they had any complaints or suggestions. I also collected money for an annual fund for employees.

Now news has just come that Mr. Pfeiffer is going to

retire on June 9. He has been with Hopmeadow right from the start, in fact Mrs. Strait tells me Mr. Pfeiffer was in on the planning and toured the country to find the very best facilities which should be included.

slip up

I went to my second Council meeting in the Sage Room, with seven Council members present plus the chef, the program director, and the chairman of the fair.

I reported that I had taken upon myself the task of visiting all the Rest Home residents. I added I was now going to have to go back again and ask for money—then I realized I'd said it right in front of Mr. Pfeiffer, from whom it was supposedly a deep, dark secret to raise funds for his retirement!

The six Council members shrieked with laughter. But I was embarrassed. I added, "I'm so Goddamned mad at myself for talking too much. Please pardon me for making such a profound error!"

Guatemala

My granddaughter, Judy, has been invited to spend the summer in Guatemala, with the family of a Wellesley classmate of my daughter. Imagine, a sixteen-year-old doing that all on her own! I don't ever remember traveling alone, except one night in Oregon when my husband left me in the care of some friends, and when I went into my hotel room all alone, I got down on my knees and checked to be sure nobody was under the bed!

There has been a dreadful earthquake in Guatemala, which may make it impossible to go, but Judy really wants to go anyway. Mildred brought me a *National Geographic* issue with an article about Guatemala.

the royal couch

Ben went shopping for me, looking for a chaise to go on my balcony, since my old one was too worn out to bring here. It arrived today, and the cushion is very puffy and bright yellow. Everyone calls it my "royal couch". Now I sit out, writing letters on the chaise. I have gone through last year's Christmas cards and selected twenty-five people I want to write to, since I didn't send out many cards last year. I have written twelve letters in ten days.

a luncheon date

It occurred to me that it would be fun to ask Jeanne and her mother-in-law to come for luncheon, so I called Jeanne and asked her if her mother-in-law, who is eighty, could walk all the way to my room, and Jeanne said, "Oh, *my* yes." Then I asked if her mother-in-law could take a sip of wine, and she said, "Oh, *my* yes!"

I invited Mildred to come at eleven o'clock, and my son Ben, and his wife, Kati, too.

The day of the luncheon I was awake at five-thirty, thinking about my plans, and I decided I might as well get up and get ready. I checked my Dubonnet supply and found I'd need to open a second bottle, which Ben had brought me from Bermuda. But my arthritic hands couldn't twist the cap off, so I rang for the nurse to ask her to open the bottle of Dubonnet.

Later, at breakfast, I told my tablemates: "I am the only Hopmeadow resident who has asked a night nurse to open a bottle at six-thirty a.m.!"

Just then I remarked about a pretty poinsettia out in the garden beyond the dining room that I hadn't seen before. This caused Lindy to ask, "Laura, how much of the

Dubonnet did you drink before breakfast? That's no pointsettia—that's a red truck behind some spruce trees!"

Guess I've got a reputation!

Ben and Kati arrived, bringing me a small, lovely watering can. It now takes only two trips to water all my plants, instead of the eight it used to take, using a little paper cup! Mrs. Osgood brought a box of delicious English biscuits. The six of us had a pleasant visit. Mrs. Osgood Sr. is English, but she grew up in West Africa, and her husband, Frank Sr., was written about in a book about Africa she loaned me. It's fascinating reading about game control work, and it even tells about Mr. Osgood getting hit with a poisoned arrow.

penny for your thoughts

Mildred asked me to take over the job of interviewing people for the Newsletter, in a column called "A penny for your thoughts". The question I had to ask this month was: "Who do you think will be the Democratic candidate for President, and why?" I saw seven people in two hours, and this is what was printed:

Stanley: "Humphrey—he is the most experienced."

Lindy: "Kennedy—I just think so."

Eva: "H.H. Humphrey—because he deserves the hassle."

Becky: "I don't know enough about any of them to form an opinion."

Thaniel: "Kennedy. I think he could do a good job and he is nice looking."

Harriet: "I like Kennedy—but I don't think he'd get it because he is too young."

Isabel: "Kennedy—because that name is magic. His morals don't mean a thing to the young people."

downstairs for Isabel

Unfortunately, Isabel took a tumble in March and broke her hip and was taken to the hospital. When she returned, about three weeks later, she had to go to a room downstairs in the medical center, and she's very unhappy because she doesn't ever expect to be able to come back to her room upstairs. I usually stop in and see her once a day, and try to cheer her up.

M A Y

Nicole comes to lecture

On one of Polly's visits we went out to see Jeanne's antique shop in Brookfield, called "The Pink Elephant." We met Nicole there, Jeanne's partner in the antique business. I was very impressed with Nicole, who was born in France, lived there for eleven years, and then went to Egypt where her father was in the French Embassy in Cairo. I invited her to come to talk one evening at Hopmeadow to the Book Review group in the Sage room.

I made all the arrangements, and called my friend Maud, to come for an overnight visit from her retirement home in Guilford, Connecticut, so she could hear Nicole.

Maud arrived early and got settled into the guest room, and then Mildred joined us for Dubonnet before supper. Twenty-five people attended the program— only up to ten had attended before. I stood up and introduced Nicole and she talked informally for an hour. A little lady I call "Miss Two Shawls", because she is always complaining of the cold, and always carries both a sweater and a shawl, but never seems to put them on, has the habit of coming in late to every meeting and is very disruptive. So I spoke to her ahead of time, and asked her

24

not to come in late. She was there on time for once, but plunk in the middle of the lecture while Nicole was telling of her life in Egypt, there was silence for a moment, and "Miss Two Shawls" started to count out loud: "Un, deux, trois," and so on, and when she got to ten, she started reciting the days of the week: "Lundi, Mardi, Mercredi. . ." I guess she wanted to impress us with her French! We had punch and a social half hour afterwards, and everyone liked it very much. Maud and I had a good visit, chatting in my room until ten.

big night out

Jeanne called and asked me to a buffet supper party at her home. I got all dressed up in my long, black skirt and embroidered blouse from Madeira, and waited to be picked up at six in the lounge. Frank wasn't home yet, though he's due very soon, but Jeanne's mother-in-law was there, Nicole and her husband, a Scottish couple, and two other couples.

I told three stories. One of the guests got very affectionate with me, and I was brought home at eleven. I needed a little help getting to my bed, after two drinks and wine with dinner. Got my light off at eleven-thirty.

behind locked doors

I find that I can play the organ with one finger, so I go in the room where it is and close the doors to make sure no one is listening.

The reason I'd like to be able to play is that I understand from people who attend the Thursday services that the lady who usually plays, can only play in the key of C. She doesn't know any sharps or flats. Of course, most of the pieces she tries to play aren't written in the key of C, so it's pretty God-awful.

The physical therapist came around and gave me some soft silly-putty to squeeze, to try to make my fingers so they'll work on the organ. It's like having a new toy!

J U N E

Mr. Pfeiffer's farewell

We held the party for Mr. Pfeiffer's farewell on June 9. On looking around our dining room, I had noticed that many of the men dress very casually, wearing just open sport shirts. So for the party, I suggested they all wear jackets and bow ties, since Mr. Pfeiffer usually wears a bow tie. It turned out that some of the men don't own a jacket, so I called Ben and arranged to get some spare jackets and bow ties.

Tessie, a nice young woman in a wheelchair downstairs, and I met four days in a row, to wrap boxes inside of boxes for Mr. Pfeiffer's gift. I passed out all the jackets and ties Ben brought. There was one gentleman who's neck was too large and heavy to get a tie around. After dinner at noon on the day of the party I put on my red linen dress and white sweater and went to the Council meeting, then changed to my black skirt and pretty blouse and prepared for guests. Four came for Dubonnet, and Lindy and Stanley stopped by in their jackets and ties for our approval.

The party went very well, with Hannah Strait saying appropriate words to convey everyone's high regard. The chef, dressed in his white coat, chef's hat and bow tie, rolled in the food cart carrying the huge wrapped box with beautiful papers and ribbons. It took Mr. Pfeiffer quite a while to get through the seven wrapped boxes inside, before he finally got to his gift, which was a check for $150 from all the residents, toward a trip he's taking.

26

During the meal I was sitting next to a very nice lady. I believe she must be on the board of directors, and I had the nerve to call her "Lydia," and, by golly, when she left she said, "Goodby, Laura!" The next day Mr. Pfeiffer stopped in at my room and we had a nice visit and he said goodby.

celebrating my eighty-first

The week before my birthday Isabel invited all the people at our table, plus three other of my friends to her room for drinks to celebrate my birthday.

On my birthday, Isabel wasn't feeling well. She missed all her meals and called the party off. Two days later she felt better, but then had to have oxygen and go to the hospital for transfusions. When she came back I visited her briefly each day, then a few days later I pushed her in her wheelchair out of doors after supper.

On Friday, June 11, we had my delayed party in Isabel's room. There were eight of us, including her daughter. Isabel was on her bed and invited me to join her since I usually entertain from my bed. It was quite a sight—the two of us, side-by-side on her bed! But I found it didn't work too well—I couldn't drink lying down! So instead I perched on Isabel's potty chair. They all sang to me and we had a jolly time.

Frank gets back from Africa

I rushed to finish the book on Africa, because Frank is back from his safari, and I was invited to dinner again to meet him.

I liked him very much. He seems a fine guy. He promised he'd talk to our group at Hopmeadow, so I wrote up the details for the Newsletter. Mrs. Osgood Sr. was there for dinner too, but she left at eight for Bingo. She goes out to play two times a week with her older friends, and often makes $5.00 a night. The Osgood's floors are covered with animal rugs. They have a nine-year old son, a new litter of German Shepherd pups, and two parrots.

new Director

I've met Mr. and Mrs. Daniel Brady, the new, young Director and his wife. He is so young, it doesn't seem possible that he could be Director and have all this responsibility.

Andy and the bet

My grandson, Andrew, picked me up today and took me to a surprise birthday party for my son, Ben, who was very surprised to find me there! Andy brought me back home at nine-thirty. He seems to get along very well with everyone—he is particularly popular with the nurses.

Isabel and I are trying to arrange a meeting between her granddaughter, who is still at college, and my grandson, who graduated last year and is working now.

I knew Andy intended to call on Mr. Brady, and I just happened to be in Mr. Brady's office when his secretary told him he'd had a call from Andrew Hunter. I said, "Gee whiz, I think I know what that's about. Are you a betting man?"

"He said, "Sure", so I said, "I'll bet you a quarter my grandson is going to make you his first policyholder."

Mr. Brady was willing, so we shook hands on it. Later we were having our monthly cocktail party outside on the patio, and it was lovely. I could see Mr. Brady through the window in his office, so I beckoned to him, and sure enough, he came out and sat down and had wine with us!

At the first Assembly meeting with Mr. Brady, he

talked while sitting down, and people couldn't see him very well, so before the next meeting I stopped in at his office and left a message for him to stand up when he spoke at the meeting.

I brought up the question of long mirrors, which I believe should be installed, because some women look like the devil, and come to meals with slips hanging down way below their dresses.

Isabel and her bequest

Isabel is now in great pain, and aching in every joint. She has had to make several trips back to the hospital for blood transfusions, and every time she returns her arm is all black and blue with bruises. She is eating very little. She hasn't been to her place at the table for several weeks, but we are still saving it for her.

A doctor once told me that most elderly people die of starvation, and I can see that is what is happening with Isabel. It certainly is no problem of mine right now. I eat enormous meals!

After Isabel last returned from the hospital she called me to come to her room and she was all propped up with pillows and looking very gaunt and frail. She told me that I was her very best friend at Hopmeadow and she wanted me to know that the doctors had given her a choice. She could go on having transfusions and live, or not have transfusions, which she hates, and die. She has decided she would rather die, since she is in constant pain. We had a cry together, and she asked me to tell the rest of our table.

I scurried around and sent messages to all the others to meet in my room at four before supper, and they all came. I told them Isabel's exact words, and about my own two children who died, and we all cried together.

Later on when some of them went to visit Isabel, she

said that she was going to bequeath her place at our table to "Miss Two Shawls". One of them responded, "Oh, Isabel, what a sweet, thoughtful thing for you to do!" But when one of the others heard that, she said, "If Isabel does that, we're all going to move."

I knew she couldn't be serious, so next time I saw her I asked if she had been kidding, and she snorted, "Of course I was!"

J U L Y

the Bicentennial and the Olympics

On July 4th I read the book on Africa on my chaise, then took a walk in the light rain, and then went to Tess's room to watch "Operation Sail", the tall sailing ships, on t.v. I saw more ads than tall ships. Two days later I watched t.v. again and saw Queen Elizabeth in Washington at dinner. Margaret and I have a 25¢ bet on. I think that Queen Elizabeth will abdicate next year, when Prince Charles becomes twenty-five.

I had a surprise visit from an old friend who is on his way from San Francisco to the Montreal 1976 Summer Olympics. He is on the Hospitality Committee for the U.S., and he brought me a personal, engraved invitation to Hospitality House in Montreal. I watched the Olympics one night in Frances Duffy's room. It turned out that my grandson, Andrew, is going to the Olympics, and I'm not, so I passed my invitation along to him. When Andy said goodby after his visit, he pinched my cheeks! I later stopped by and paid Mr. Brady a quarter, because Andy has already sold a policy to someone else. Mr. Brady gave me a signed receipt.

30

an African evening

The day arrived for Frank's visit. I talked it up, and invited several guests, including my grandsons Andy and Alex, to usher. The Osgoods came at six-thirty, and Andy and Alex arrived with a fresh supply of Dubonnet and an ice chest full of beer. Frank started to talk about seven o'clock. Fifty people were present in the Sage Room, the most we have ever had come for any talk. They had to leave aisles open for the wheelchairs. Frank talked informally about his background and work on safaris and then showed slides of people and animals for over an hour. Andy and Alex served the punch, and some cookies one of the girls had made, while everyone chatted. Then three couples, and Andy and Alex, came to my room for Dubonnet and beer.

There was much chatter going on, and then the phone rang. It was Alice Eldred, a friend of seventy years ago, whom I hadn't talked to in forty years. I shushed up all the guests, and said to her: "Can you call back tomorrow? I have ten guests in here, all drinking!" Uproarious laughter! My light went off at ten; the nurses were most cooperative. It was a perfectly splendid evening.

General Brewster and the Queen

I received in the mail a gorgeous photograph of Queen Elizabeth with my friend, General Sir John Brewster. It was signed, "Love from both of us." In the background I can just catch a glimpse of Brewster's wife, Rosemary, but it made it look like it was love from the Queen!

John's letter explained this was taken at his retirement dinner "with one of my girlfriends."

I took the photo to dinner and passed it around, and asked everyone if they knew who the picture was of, and they all recognized the Queen, but didn't know who the man was.

I explained the whole story about my husband meeting John at the army base, when John was teaching the American soldiers desert warfare, and how he and his wife came to stay for a short visit before their return to England, and spent three weeks. They had to wait for a ship with a doctor on board, since Rosemary was eight months pregnant. We had a good time waiting together. They finally joined a convoy and arrived back in England safely, and when their daughter was born soon after, they asked me to be Godmother.

After dinner I took the photograph down to Isabel's room and she knew right off it was the Queen. Isabel is thin as a rail and not eating a bite, but she is as spunky as ever. I kissed her goodnight and she told me she loved me. I went to my room feeling very sad and teary, and Julie comforted me.

A U G U S T

slipped drawers

While we were still sitting around our table in the dining room after noonday dinner, Hannah Strait, the Hopmeadow founder's niece and Council Chairman, was slowly shuffling out of the dining room—she uses one cane—and all of a sudden Charlie, one of the last people in the dining room, sitting alone at another table, let out a hoot, and we all looked up and saw that Hannah had dropped her panties down around her ankles! Everyone howled with laughter, and Hannah's was the greatest laugh of all. She repaired to the privacy of the gallery, and soon had everything under control.

To Laura Hunter
with love from us both
John

After supper that night I put on a sweater and walked outside. I stopped by where Hannah was sitting to say,"I hope the elasticity in your undergarments is secure!" She has a marvelous good humor.

the podiatrist

The podiatrist came, and worked on my feet. I said "Ouch!" so often he said I was being dramatic, and asked me, "Have you ever been an actress?" I said, "If you give me a pair of scissors I'll cut your toenails and see if you don't say "Ouch!" Every time he comes in, he says "Helleluia!", so I say "Helleluia" back. He charges $12, which is more than the other podiatrist I had, he hurts more, and he takes less time.

in the mailbox

I received a letter from my granddaughter, Judy, who is now in Guatemala, attending school. Their school year is different from ours since their winter is our summer.

Judy wrote:

> Dear Granny,
>
> I'm having a fantastic time (down) here in Guatemala. It's almost as though I'm an entirely new and different person living (starting) an entirely different life.
>
> The first few days in colegio Monte Maria I was so nervous that about all I could do was smile a huge grin and say "Hola" (hi) ten million times. I think now I must be friends with *every* single kid in the school (maybe not the teachers), but the circle of people I know keeps widening.
>
> We went to Antigua, the old capital of Guatemala. There's quite a bit of damage from the earthquake still, but mostly it's very pretty. From there we

34

went to the finca (farm), which is between two volcanos. I don't know what I expected, but it is huge, a whole town, with people, houses, dogs, chickens, cows, a school, church and medical center. I tried my hand at milking. I fell in love with the kitchen—a big, dark room mostly filled with huge pilas, no ceiling, just open at one end, and they were making delicious cheese tortillas.

Last Saturday I attended a "noche alegre" (happy night) party for our grade. In the course of the night they sang two chants or songs praising me—that made me feel pretty good! It was a happy night, and I didn't sleep much so to make up for it I slept all yesterday.

I would like to bring home a parrot, but I won't be here long enough to have owned it for the required three months. We are going shopping soon so I can buy something for each of you at home.

Lots of love, Juanita

I also received a request from President Ford for support for his presidential campaign, so I sent in $10, since I wouldn't want to see Jimmy Carter President.

wallowing olympic champion

We were invited for a swim at the family pool of a Norwegian lady who lives at Hopmeadow. Patrick, a young man from here, played on an inflated dragon, and Tessie was lifted in from her wheelchair. They called me the "olympic champion", because I can really swim, and I love it.

I went to Polly's home for three days during an unusual August spell when it was beautiful weather and not too hot. She took me swimming twice at her friend's pool—part of a very practical new condominium. I swam

35

the whole length of the pool twice, but at one point I wallowed, and couldn't tell which way was up. Fortunately Polly was right there and saved me.

misplaced sympathy

I was waiting for pills one morning, and the assistant head nurse, who's fairly new, came up and sat beside me, and put her hand on my lap, and very sympathetically said, "your husband is better and will be home by Wednesday."

I looked at her in great amazement, and said,

"That is most unlikely, as my husband has been gone for ten years!" Poor thing, she didn't realize there were two Mrs. Hunters here.

We've fortunately found a new podiatrist, who's much nicer than the old one. At breakfast Louise was talking about him, and commented that he has six children. Hannah immediately asked, "Where did he get his training?" More laughs!

Payson paid his usual Thursday visit and brought me several things I'd requested: an address book, a new clock, since my old one gave up on me, and a magnifying glass. This helps, since my left eye isn't much good.

Jeanne called to say they are going to move to Texas, because they think New England is too cold and they don't like our snow. I'll be sorry to see them go. But I've invited Frank to come and talk again before they go.

a gift of scrimshaw

Warren Schoonmaker, from Cardinal Life, came to visit, and brought a booklet commemorating the one hundred and twenty-fifth anniversary of both my father's and my husband's insurance company. He brought me a gift of scrimshaw: a cardinal etched on a piece of whalebone, hung on a gold chain. I asked everyone at my table if they knew what scrimshaw is. No one there did, but Mildred knew when I asked her. I knew, because my grandfather, Benjamin Franklin Russell, was from Nantucket, and I'd heard lots of tales about whaling.

Isabel takes a turn

Sunday morning I was at breakfast and I saw Isabel's daughter come rushing in. I thought surely something had happened. As soon as I could I left the table and went down to Isabel's room, expecting the worst. I went in and there I found Isabel—exuberant! Her daughter had brought her sausage and French pancakes, still piping hot. It's something she can't get here, and she had devoured every scrap. Later, I went to her room to have her sign a card from everyone at our table for Lindy's father, who's very ill. She was sitting on the porch—feeling much better without so much medicine.

I decided to give a party, and asked a few people in for drinks. Izzie came upstairs in her wheelchair, bringing a new bottle of wine. By golly, there we all were, and in comes Mr. Brady!

"I heard there's a party up here", he says. There wasn't another chair, so I said, "I'll share my bed with you. At least you can sit on the edge!"

He didn't sit, but he did have some of Lindy's diet-ginger to drink.

This week I also entertained Mr. and Mrs. Berry and Mildred, each of whom I owed a drink, so at the moment I don't owe anybody anything.

a race with Mil

Mildred has been having some heart trouble, so she has moved downstairs, and uses a wheelchair some of the time. We have a race, to see who gets to breakfast first.

"Be careful," I tell her, as she wheels around. "I don't want you to be reckless!"

"I don't need a traffic manager," she says.

breakfast laughs

When I arrived at the table one morning, I announced: "I HAD A DREAM!" It was about Mr. Brady, and we had hysterics in the dining room.

I condemned the kitchen for the awful taste of the oatmeal, until I found that I'd used pepper instead of salt! Then Lindy gave me the dickens for soaking my bathrobe sleeve in my coffee cup. But our funniest laugh, which really shouldn't have been funny at all, but I guess we were all being silly, was the news about the suffering, bedridden lady who had died in the night. When Penny, our waitress, heard that, she said: "Oh, no *wonder* she didn't send for her breakfast!"

S E P T E M B E R

will Isabel make it to the Fair?

Isabel asked me if there was anything of hers that I'd like, and I said, "Sure, I'd like a third of your fortune." (I wanted her to know I think she's quite wealthy!) She gave me another handsewn purse of Evie's, slightly larger than the one I have, because she thought my old one was soiled.

Isabel has been made the honorary chairman of the Fair, since it was her idea. Everyone is busy collecting rummage, making quilts and sewing in the crafts room.

We are all hoping Isabel will be at the Fair, since it was her idea, but we can't help wondering if she will make it, she is eating so little.

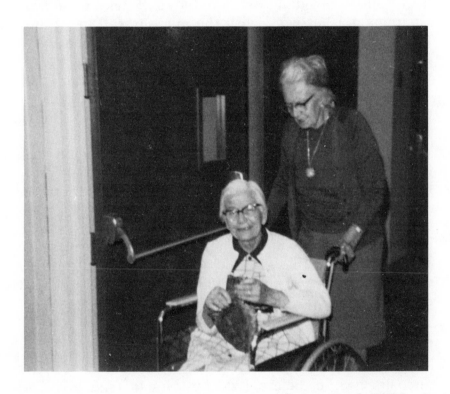

Laura with Mildred

But she says: Don't worry, I swear I'll be there. . .I'm going to be collecting all that money at the cashier's desk."

gratitude

I visited my daughter for Judy's homecoming from Guatemala. I left word with the nurse to call me if anything happens to Isabel. Down at Polly's I woke up at five-thirty and wrote in my journal, and found myself weeping with happiness, everyone is so good to me. There were flowers on my breakfast tray, and Judy brought me pretty painted birds from Guatemala, which I've hung from my lamp.

I got back Friday, and the Fair started at one o'clock Saturday. The rains, which threatened, held off, and mobs of people were milling around. I bought three aprons for my daughter and two daughters-in-law, a tiny, hand-dressed doll for my youngest granddaughter, my second namesake, and a smocked dress for the next youngest. Isabel was there like she said she would be, and the Fair was a great success. About $4,000 was raised, a good start on the van.

after supper routine

After supper there's a group of us that usually collects and sits awhile, before I go upstairs to read my *Wall Street Journal*. They all think I must have lots of stocks that I should want to read the *Journal*, but I just like to know what the market is doing, and I sometimes catch little items about people I know.

There's a man I've seen now every day in the lounge for six months, who has never said a word. He is tied into his wheelchair, and is always bent way over so you really don't see his face.

40

As I approached this time, I could see there weren't enough chairs for us all, and a man nearby offered to bring up another one. Suddenly the man in the wheel-chair lifted his head up and said with the nicest smile:

"You can sit in my lap if you like!"

stranger from Shady Lane

I usually wake up at two o'clock in the morning and I call the nurse the help me get to the john, to be sure I don't fall. The night nurse, who has a Belgian name, was looking at all the post cards which I have taped up all around my room from all over the world, and she recognized the card of Table Mountain, in Cape Town, South Africa, that had come from Nan, the American Field Service student who lived with Polly's family for a year.

The nurse told me there is a family from Cape Town on her street, Shady Lane, in Brookfield. I said, "I'd like to get in touch with them," so she gave me their name.

At nine-thirty in the morning I looked them up in the phone book and gathered my courage and called. An English-sounding gentleman answered, and said he was visiting from Cape Town. He seemed very interested in seeing and talking with me when I said I had two friends in Cape Town. He said he'd call back when his hostess returned and tell me if he could come over. He called back later and accepted an invitation to come at three.

I told my friends at lunch that this strange man from Shady Lane was coming to visit me. It made a very good story. They thought I should be chaperoned, so I asked Lindy to stop by and meet him.

Clive arrived promptly at three o'clock. He is twenty-seven, bearded, with longish hair and a great handshake. He brought beautiful pictures of Cape Town for me to see. We chatted for about an hour and finished up the last of a bottle of Dubonnet. Lindy dropped in and Clive's hostess came for a minute. Clive is several generations South African, and on his way to England tomorrow to see the tennis matches.

It was great fun having this happen, all as a result of a trip to the john in the middle of the night.

Ford-Carter debates

I stayed up until 10:30 one night to watch the Ford-Carter debate. Next day I received a letter from the White House thanking me for my $10 gift. There were two pictures enclosed of President Ford. I taped them up on my closet door along with lots of other cards and pictures, and bragged to my friends about being the only one to receive a letter from the White House.

After supper one evening I took a walk, and I told the ladies they could be excused, as Lindy and I could get along together! I ended up with a good visit with Isabel. Mildred had a dizzy spell and a sharp pain, so she didn't come to supper. I left word with the nurse that I wanted to be called day or night if she needed someone, as she has no relatives near.

Mildred's niece

Mildred has no children, but she has a niece, Lesley, who lives in the family house in the Adirondacks with her third husband. Lesley is in her sixties and the new husband is eighty, a great big, husky fellow. They visited Mildred recently, and she invited me to meet them. We warmed up very fast, so I invited them back to my room for a drink before dinner. He came in with arms outstretched, and gave me two, great, big kisses. I didn't pour as much Dubonnet for me as I did for him. Mildred got upset and thought I egged him on. I assured her later that it was all quite innocent!

egg consumption

Speaking of eggs, at breakfast one day I told my tablemates how, for twenty-five years, I had a man who opened my boiled egg for me at breakfast. I never had to do it except when he was on vacation, and then I didn't eat eggs. At Hopmeadow the waitress doesn't open my boiled egg, so I make a stab at it. Just as I was talking, I found a piece of shell in my mouth!

This started a conversation about how many eggs everyone eats. This spread around the dining room, and pretty soon everyone was asking each other, "How many eggs do you eat?"

Some said, "None, they're bad for me. Too much cholesterol."

It turned out that I eat more than anyone else. I eat two for breakfast, one in a morning eggnog, and one in an afternoon eggnog, or twenty-eight in a week! Everyone thought that was excessive. So now it's been cut down to seven.

the hairdresser

Mildred and I were both at the hairdresser this afternoon, when Mr. Brady stopped in (I looked my worst!), and he said, "I knew you girls would be together!"

Later we went to my room, and Mildred turned down a drink, saying, "I'm on the wagon." I asked if that was because she'd had too much yesterday, to which she replied, "I don't have to answer you."

Mil fills her birdfeeder with thistleseeds, and we got to laughing, trying to say "thistleseeds", without lisping.

new "patron"

We have a new "patron" at our table—Hannah Strait. So now I have to be on my best behavior. She and her sister are being separated, since they spend a lot of time together anyway, with Hannah reading to her and keeping her company. They switched Grace to another table; I'm glad they didn't switch me. Lindy and I have quite a time!

O C T O B E R

the weather chills

Mr. Brady caught up with me in the corridor after breakfast one morning. He showed me how cold it was by giving me his hand to warm up. Mildred was an onlooker, and I'm not sure she approved.

There are plans afoot for enlarging Hopmeadow by adding apartments. I'm very opposed to adding anything, because the present size is perfect. One hundred people is just enough for everyone to know each other.

They would have to cut down a lot of trees, and I'm working instead to have them build a swimming pool. It wouldn't cost nearly as much, though of course it wouldn't be income-producing like the apartments would.

I told Mr. Brady I wanted a swimming pool, and he gave me a four page report to read on solar dome pools for the elderly. He suggested I report on it to the Board of Directors. If they're going to have it, I'd like them to have it while I'm around, so I could use it.

Another time I met Mr. Brady in the corridor, and he remarked how pretty my hair looked. That set me up for the day! Someday I think I'm going to call him "Daniel".

I investigated the Blue Spruce Grove progress for Isabel and reported back to her, then after dinner I pushed her in her wheelchair out to see the new paths, which have just been blacktopped. They weren't quite ready, but I pushed the front wheels of her chair on it, so she would be the first to use it.

African animals

Frank came back a second time, on my request, and brought a friend, Tom, an artist, who has painted many pictures of African animals, based on Frank's photographs. Frank played tapes of the sounds of African animals, while we sat and looked at Tom's paintings, and then Frank answered more questions about Africa. I'm going to see if Tom can exhibit his work in the gallery downstairs. Perhaps he'll sell something!

my biggest day

As a farewell party, I invited Frank and Jeanne to dinner at the Brookfield Club, along with his mother and their son, Eric, and my son Ben, with Kati and the Swifts. I invited my son, Jonathan, and Polly, too, with their spouses, but they couldn't come. It was my biggest day yet, including an exercise class at ten-thirty, shampoo at two, to the lounge at three-forty-five for the monthly cocktail party, then at five-thirty to Ben and Kati's for drinks before dinner at the Club. It was a good dinner, and Frank said it was the best food he'd had in the United States!

Home at ten-forty, with two nurses helping me undress. A great eve.

Jeanne called to say goodby the morning they left for Fort Worth, all packed up in their car and a rented van.

A week later, I read in the paper that the only place in

the United States on November 13 to have snow was Fort Worth! I wrote Jeanne a letter saying they'd picked the wrong spot to go to get away from the snow!

N O V E M B E R

"Settled By The Sea"

I started reading the book *Settled by the Sea*, by Lemuel Howorth, who wrote a number of poems and books. I remembered that Lemuel Howorth was someone whom Maud had had a crush on, in fact I suspected she was in love with him, as I knew she had visited him several times, so I wrote and asked if I were right. I added a big DAMN when I heard the results of the election at five-thirty a.m. President Ford lost to Jimmy Carter!

A week later I received a six page letter, and I was right! Maud confides she *did* love Lemuel Howorth, and she told me of each of the five times she saw him, and about the love letters he wrote to her (which Lemuel's wife didn't see), and the proper letters she wrote to him, which his wife *did* see. Maud enclosed a copy of a very lovely little poem Lemuel wrote her, and said she will burn his letters someday. Here is the poem she enclosed:

> Regard this compass
> How veeringly the needle turns,
> Yet ever northward yearns.
> And at the last will come
> Faithfully home.
> Even so my love
> Resembles
> The needle, for it turns to you
> And trembles.

Mr. O'Mara wanders

The nurse told me at five a.m. that dear old Alfie kept Mildred awake all night! He entered her room four times during the night. Mildred finally got up in her nighty, put on a white shawl, and took him down the corridor to his room.

The next night Alfie got out the back door somehow and was found wandering in the woods. Now they have a male aid all day and night to keep an eye on him. He really is a dignified, nice man, very well dressed. He sits in a chair, with his head in his hands, looking like death itself, but when I arrive, he jumps up and offers me his chair!

After I've finished my morning drink, he takes the empty cup to the snack bar, rinses it out, like we're supposed to do, and puts it on the cart to go to the kitchen. He's a perfectly lovely gentleman, whom I think deserves a poem or a song.

the "Grand Young Dame"

Hannah Strait's birthday was today, so at noontime when the dining room was filled, Joyce brought in a cake with one lighted candle. Archie and all the kitchen help and waitresses all came in as I stood, pounded my knife on a coffee cup and waited a full, half minute until all was quiet. Then I said in a loud, clear voice: "It seems very fitting at this moment to all sing "Happy Birthday" to Hannah Strait, who, as the 'Grand *Young* Dame' of Hopmeadow Home, is celebrating her 90th birthday today."

Everyone sang and Hannah rose and said "Thank you." I told her later that I was determined to get the "damn" in somewhere.

The same afternoon all our table went to Grace's room

to celebrate Hannah's birthday. I wore my schrimshaw necklace, and also a pair of ivory carved earrings that I've never worn very much before, but which go well with the necklace.

I've begun work on a poem, called "O'Mara and Me." I work on it when I wake up, first thing in the morning.

D E C E M B E R

an invitation to snowmobile

Frank's friend, Tom, came at eleven-thirty to my room for Dubonnet, and then he joined our table for lunch, along with Isabel, who gets to the table now and then. I got up during lunch and introduced Tom, so everybody would stop and see his animal paintings which are now hung in the gallery, on their way out of the dining room. After lunch, when Tom had left, I took a walk. It was almost dark, with snowflakes in the air.

Next day I had a call from Tom. He said the nicest things that made my day! He'd heard from Frank and Jeanne, and all is well in Texas. Tom says he'll take me for a ride on his snowmobile! I've told everybody I have an invitation, and Hannah is going to loan me her warm underwear!

"Miss Two Shawls" stopped by at our table today to say she should have a kick in the pants—and I volunteered to give it to her!

I walked out with Isabel in the sun, at 20°. It was lovely. Then I went to exercise class, and had a shampoo, hair cut and manicure in the afternoon. Mr. Brady came by the day room this morning and I tempted him to join us for Ann Landers, but he turned it down, blushing.

elephant stew

Nicole sent me this recipe with the note: "Here is a recipe for cook, next time I come to lunch. It should not be too much trouble." I had Joyce, Penny and Archy, the chef, read it.

Elephant Stew

1 elephant
salt and pepper
2 rabbits
Cut elephant into small, bite-sized pieces.
This should take about two months. Add enough brown gravy to cover. Cook over kerosene fire about four weeks at 450°. This will serve about 3800 people. If more are expected, two rabbits may be added, but only if necessary, as most people do not like to find 'hare' in their stew.

(Juan Armour)

The next day after breakfast, Mr. Brady came up behind me and poked me in the back, and I said, "You're just the man I want to see. I have something for you, to take to your wife, Gretchen, in case she's wondering what to have for Christmas." Then I gave him a copy I'd made of "Elephant Stew." I told him I'd also given it to Archy, but that Archy said he'd have to go to Africa to get the ingredients, and I said he'd have to take me along as well.

Jeanne wrote from Texas that they did indeed have snow, but that it didn't last long. Frank is in the Sudan, Jeanne has a job in a game coin shop, with lovely animal paintings, prints and jewelry and other African artifacts, Eric is busy fishing, and Frank's mother has won $50 at bingo!

I'm working on the poem, "O'Mara and Me", putting it to music. When Polly called, I sang it to her and to Judy, and she said she'd send me a page of a blank music book, with staff lines, so I can write out the music properly.

letters to the living

I have an old friend, in California, whose wife died several years ago. I decided I'd write to him, as well as to several others I haven't heard from in a long time, to see if they are still living. I have a photograph of the four of us, my husband and I, Douglas and Catherine, skiing at Lake Placid fifty-two years ago, when Catherine and I were both pregnant. Skiing was a brand new sport, and we were all very brave, going out on our long hickory slats!

Douglas now lives in a nine-story retirement home in Santa Barbara. When I wrote him, he wrote right back. Then three days later he wrote me another letter—which said exactly the same things!

I have a secret

I have been reading the *Reader's Digest*, and now I've found it in big print, which is especially good. I wrote up my two pet stories (the frozen valve one, and "in the shape of Laura Winslow") and sent them off to *Reader's Digest*. They're surely as funny as some that are printed in "Life in These United States." I decided to keep it a secret and wait until I get a check in the mail, and then I'll come to the table and show my secret with a $200 check or two.

Now everyone wants to know my secret. I called Polly, Jonathan and Ben and told each of them I have a secret in the mail!! It's causing lots of good fun.

My tablemates decided one morning that the "secret" is that I'm going to get married! So the four women at my table resolved to be bridesmaids, and Lindy the ring-bearer. This led at lunch to the five women all telling of

Lake Placid, 1926

our first meeting our husbands. I met Gordon at the Hartford YMCA, when I as playing the cornet with an all-girl band. Dusty Preston played the violin, Molly Burns the drums, and Phyllis Kielty the piano. Gordon was a salesman at Cardinal Life. It turned out that he was working for my father!

Christmas celebrations

I went to Polly's for Christmas, and while there I continued working on my song. So far, it's:

Alfie and me
Fine gentleman he
He looks so asleep
With never a peep
He jumps when I come
He's really quite fun

When I got back home at 8 o'clock Christmas night after starting the day with presents and breakfast in bed in Greenwich, a two hour drive, the afternoon at Ben's sleeping on the couch, then egg nog, dinner and wine and more presents, Alfie greeted me at the door of Hopmeadow with a fine handshake and a New Year's wish. He and Lindy and Stanley were all so friendly I almost cried with joy! What a lovely day!

Later I finished up the poem. The rest of it now goes:

He gives me his chair
With really a flair
And then when I drink
He goes to the sink
My cup in his hand
He's quite a nice man
He's been the world over

Christmas with grandchildren, 1976

From China to Dover
He's smart as can be
Three cheers for Alfie!

I collected Alfie, Mildred, and Julie, and I got Alfie to sit very close, so he could hear, and I sang "Alfie and Me" to him. Later I sent my sister, Florence, a copy of my poem and the recipe for Elephant Stew.

dedication service

Every day all fall I've pushed Isabel whenever she felt well enough, out to see her recreation grove. We often go out in the cold, which we both love, but everyone else is saying: "Don't go out! It's too cold!" But we have marvelous visits.

Right after Christmas Isabel invited me to a dedication service for Blue Spruce Grove. She invited her minister, Mr. Brady, her daughter, and me. It was held in her room, she in bed. It was very simple—just a couple of prayers, and some words of dedication. Then we had a drink and I found that the young minister was a nephew of the best man at our wedding in 1917!"

J A N U A R Y

the Gilmour connection

One day I was chatting with Mildred, and she mentioned her brother, Gilmour, who lives in Cambridge. I said, "Gilmour? By golly, I have a whole family of Gilmours who lived in the Boston area. I'll bet we're related!"

So I asked my sister, Miriam, to check into the family records at Nantucket where the Russells all came from. She produced a photograph, we figure it must have been taken seventy-one years ago, in 1905, since Miriam was

54

Singing to Alfie

one year old at the time. I must have been ten. It was taken at my grandparents' fiftieth wedding anniversary, with nineteen members of the family, including me and Ralph Gilmour.

Mildred denies any family connection, but when her niece was visiting Hopmeadow from Boston, we told her about my relatives and on her own initiative, she looked up the Gilmours in the phone book, and found the only Gilmour in the book, and called him and told him about meeting me in Brookfield, and he said, "Yes, I remember my Uncle Ben had a daughter, Laura, and I'd be delighted to hear from her." So I wrote him and a week later I got a reply:

"Dear Cousin Laura. . ."

Maybe he'll come to visit!

silly shenanigans

To keep my legs working, on the way to breakfast some mornings I walk all the way along the second floor, past the elevator, to the balcony, which overlooks the lounge, and go down the circular staircase.

One morning I worked my way down, as usual, a stair at a time, both canes in one hand and holding onto the rail with the other. As I neared the bottom step, Alfie was right there and helped me down.

Going into the dining room, I passed Ray Webster, who called me "Honey-bunch", so I greet him now with "Sweetie-pie" and every morning I blow kisses to him when I reach my breakfast table—and I usually get one back! Not to be outdone, I think, Hannah has joined in the fun and now she blows kisses to him too. One morning we got so silly with these shenanigans with Ray that I even made him a honey sandwich and sent it by the waitress! We keep them laughing! Frances shakes her head when

56

Nantucket, 1905

she goes by, and says to me, "You rascal!" Perhaps we're not behaving ourselves too well.

breakfast in bed—without the salt

I fell and had to stay in bed one morning. It was nice having breakfast in bed, except they forgot the salt, pepper, sugar, butter and milk! Hannah stopped in afterwards and said breakfast at the table was very dull because I wasn't there.

letter to Jimmy

I wrote a letter to President Jimmy Carter about two vital subjects. I objected about both the continuing use of his first name, Jimmy, as very childish and inappropriate for the President, and also his poor taste, in addressing the people of this country on television, in wearing a sweater instead of a well-groomed dark suit and tie, as befits a gentleman in that position.

who's smarter?

We've heard about a recent play and show on television in which Julie Harris portrays Emily Dickinson. Mildred said something which sounded to me as though she thought Emily Dickinson had died quite recently, so I told her, "Emily Dickinson has been dead some time."

"I knew that," she retorted.

"Well," I admitted, "You're much smarter than I am."

"I've always known that," she replied.

What do you do with such a smug friend?

FEBRUARY

valentines

As a project for Valentine's Day, I used some of my old note paper, and thought up ten different words to rhyme with valentine, one for each of my ten grandchildren, and mailed them off. Four of them replied, and I received quite a few other cards and letters as well.

Thinking of valentines and all, Stanley seems to be quite enamoured of an Indian nurse, who dresses in a long, flowing, white sari. She's very pretty and graceful.

South Africa and snowflakes

After reading about South Africa for the Great Decisions book club, (it's summer in South Africa now), I bundled into my heavy tweed coat, boots and two scarves, and went outside for a walk before lunch in the snow. The snowflakes falling on my face were cool and delightful. When I went back inside for lunch, they told me that everyone in the dining room had clapped when they saw me outside. Later, Mr. Brady went up on the elevator with me and called me "the most outdoors person here."

mode of departure

Mrs. Nilsson always kept Mrs. Collins company, until Mrs. Collins died about four months ago. A few days ago Mrs. Nilsson suffered a stroke at dinner. I was sitting in the lounge in the afternoon when I saw her being taken out. So now I know how you leave this place!

a radical Granny?

My grandson, Andrew, was asked to speak to one-hundred-fifty people about estate planning, and I heard from Ben he did a very good job. Andy stopped in to see me before going to San Francisco on a vacation. I told him to be sure not to miss the Top O' the Mark, and gave him his cousin Laura's address at Stanford University.

It wasn't too long before a letter arrived from Laura. She wrote:

> Dear Granny,
> Just had the pleasure of Andy's visit... We dashed over to the coast for a long stroll along the Pacific, and then came back to Columbae House for an interesting vegetarian dinner and house meeting. Andy spent the night in my room (with my three roommates!) and I slept on the roof.
> I called your friend's son, Dr. Barnum, and was invited to their home for dinner. We laughed at old pictures of you cross-country skiing at Lake Placid. I hope to ski at Yosemite this winter.
> I'm applying to live next year in a new theme house I've helped to organize, called "Androgyny House." Do you know what that word means?
>
> > Much love,
> > Laura
>
> P.S. Andy and I decided you are the most radical (crazy, playful) member of the family. Congrats.

the androgyny mystery

That word, androgyny, is a totally new word to me. I didn't have the faintest idea as to its meaning. I tried it out on my breakfast companions, and Lindy, as it turns out, came the closest, with "a mixture of the sexes." Even Mildred didn't know what it meant. We wondered why they would name a house for it, so I called up Laura to ask her, so I could tell my friends. She explained that young men and women live in the house, all cooking their

60

own meals, with lots of discussions and meetings on the subject of sex roles and how they can change them so men don't *have* to be strong and competitive and logical, and women delicate and nurturing and emotional, but they can combine them.

We're not sure what to make of all that.

This week's church service was conducted by a nice young woman minister, named Brenda, whom Millie and I went to hear. We two are considered heathens, because we generally don't go to church. (I don't go, because the pews are just too damn hard!) After the service, the minister sat at our table for luncheon, so I asked her if *she* knew the word "androgyny," and she did.

As I look around the dining room, I think the most "androgynous" person here is "Harry", but then perhaps we all get more androgynous as we age.

M A R C H

the damn hassock

We were all in place in the lounge for an Assembly meeting when a call came for me that the dentist had arrived and wanted to see me. I got up and tripped over the big hassock, which I didn't see, and I fell and hit my head on the floor. People rushed to pick me up and as they got me on my feet everybody clapped. I said, "Damn!" and the nurse said, "She's alright!"

bouillabaise

I was invited out to friends of the Osgoods in West Brookfield for dinner. I knew it would be late, and everyone said I should eat at five o'clock with my regular table. Afterwards I waited in the lounge for Nicole till six-forty-five. She and her husband, Ted, took me to the Martins' for drinks and a delicious dinner. Tom Martin is a great big fella, with just as big hugs. In the center of the dining table was a lovely, huge, old English soup tureen, filled with lobster, crabmeat, clams, mussels and fish, all served with a big soup ladle. It's called bouillabaise, and it was the first time I'd ever had it. Conversation kept going till eleven, when Nicole and Ted brought me home, back up to my room. I was so exhilarated I hardly slept.

At breakfast next morning Hannah didn't know what bouillabaise was, but Fanny, being a nutritionist, did. We had a great discussion as to the spelling of bouillabaise— and I won. Mildred looked it up in her dictionary.

After breakfast I bumped into Mr. Brady on the second floor. He threatened to put me on a curfew, because of my late night!

Livingstone and Stanley Steamers

We had another great breakfast discussion, this one about the source of the Nile River. We talked about Livingstone, who had something to do with Africa, but I wasn't sure what. I thought they said his name was Stanley Livingstone. Somehow we got all mixed up, and talking about the Stanley Steamer, started by two brothers, twins, famous people born in Maine, whom I'd been reading about. It was all so ridiculously funny we were in stitches.

Lindy's dream

We're getting ready for a Scandinavian party with a Scandinavian menu, and we're all supposed to dress appropriately for the occasion. Meg showed slides of her trip to Scandinavia, to get us in the mood. I talked to Kati about borrowing a shawl she crocheted, it's really a poncho, that goes on over the head, that I remembered seeing her wear, made up of all different colored squares. Lindy says a poncho is not Scandinavian, but Mexican. Later Lindy told us the funniest story—he said it wasn't really a dream, it was a thought (I suspected it was while he was on the toilet), of the Scandinavian dinner all mixed up with me in a poncho driving a Stanley Steamer. Even Lindy laughed so much he was crying.

We had our Scandinavian dinner, which was a great success, and our table won the prize for the best costumes. A photographer took a picture of Joyce and me, and it was printed next day with the caption "Mrs. Lora Hunter, a patient at Hopmeadow Home. . ." I was mad at having my name misspelled, but even more, at being called a "patient." Ben knew the photographer, so I called him up and raised hell over the proper spelling of my name and I told him, "I am not a patient at Hopmeadow."

He said, "Well, you take pills, don't you?"

I argued, "Yes, but I can take pills in my own home, and that doesn't make me a patient. We would prefer to be called 'members' of Hopmeadow."

The next day Lindy said to me, "Laura, you're changing the world. You're in the paper again this morning, they printed a correction, with your right name this time."

international scene

This morning a young girl came in to my room and I said to her, "You're from the Far East." She is a Chinese girl in training from Taiwan, who studied in Germany. She's just as nice as can be. We have a very international place, with someone from India and someone from China.

I learned from my daughter that the student from South Africa who lived with them for a year, is now baby sitting for a family in Ipswich, Massachusetts, and they just had a new baby. Nan, the girl from South Africa, suggested that they name her Laura, after her adopted U.S. sister and grandmother, and sure enough, they liked the name and so they did! My friends here think it's a great joke to have a girl from South Africa living in Ipswich naming a girl after me!

major fundraiser

I read in the paper that Aetna Life gave $500 to Hopmeadow Home toward the purchase of our minibus, and I thought, if Aetna can make a donation, Cardinal Life might also. I wrote to the President of the company and told him nothing would make me happier than to have them make a gift in memory of my father and husband, both of whom gave their business years to the Agency Department of Cardinal Life, and that I have had more years as a Cardinal daughter and wife than any other person—my entire life.

A reply came from my friend, Warren, who is chairman of the Contributions Committee. They approved a gift of $250! Guess I'm not such a bad fundraiser!

Hannah flies west

Hannah is flying out to California to visit her daughter, whose husband is curator of a museum. I wrote a card with a poem, and everyone at our table signed it.

Before she left, Charles, the new President of the Council, presented Hannah with a corsage, for having finished her term as Chairman. Charles and I bought it from a florist who gives a discount to elderly citizens. That's one time we didn't object to being elderly!

St. Patrick's Day

On St. Patrick's Day, I saw Mr. Brady through the glass doors to the office. He was wearing a big pin, "Kiss Me, I'm Irish", and I told him I would have, if the glass hadn't been between him and me. I've decided he belongs in Hollywood. He's awfully good looking.

absent-minded artist

At lunch, Hannah told the story about her sister, Martha, who is now ninety-six. She has been spending quite a bit of time in the arts and crafts room, painting pictures. There is presently an exhibit, hanging in the gallery, of residents' paintings. They are all on sale for $5.00, proceeds to go toward the Fair and buying the minibus. Among the paintings is one of Martha's, a scene of a meadow with a river flowing through; as Hannah says, "conveying a very nice motion."

Hannah and Martha were sitting in the gallery together, waiting for lunch, and Martha gazed around at the paintings. She pointed to her meadow, and said to Hannah: "I certainly could have painted that scene just as well as the artist did." And Hannah replied, "But Martha, you *did* paint that picture!"

Hannah wrote the story to Martha's husband, who lives at their home still, and to whom Hannah writes almost every day, and he promptly sent $5.00 for its purchase.

the Jubilee

For the Silver Jubilee, I wanted to give a program of all my colored slides taken at the Trooping of the Color and the Queen's Coronation in 1953, but I find I can't see the pictures projected on the screen well enough to tell people about them, so I've abandoned the project.

A lovely book came from the Brewsters in England, with beautiful pictures, commemorating the Silver Jubilee. It doesn't seem twenty-five years ago, my husband and I were at Sea Island, Georgia, for an insurance convention. News came on the radio that George VI had died. I turned to Gordon and said, "There's going to be a Coronation. Let's go!"

A P R I L   A N D   M A Y

final entries

For no reason at all I've taken two more falls, and had to stay in bed for several days. My room seems to be getting darker, and I have trouble finding my shoes to slip into.

I was halfway down the hall the other day before Julie spotted me with one black and one red shoe on, and sent me back to change.

A letter arrived from my grandson, Paul. He's in jail, at the Manchester Armory in New Hampshire. I've been hearing on the radio, about the nuclear plant at Seabrook, New Hampshire, where over a thousand people were arrested and hauled away by the police. It worries me, but I'm feeling punk and I'm just too tired to think about it.

I wrote Isabel a note, since I don't have the energy to go see her. The next morning I heard she'd died. I'll never know if she got my note.

I heard a woodpecker for the first time this spring. . .

*   *   *

Mildred came around collecting new quotes for the newsletter. This time her question was "What is your recipe for Happiness?"

Mine just popped right out, without my even stopping to think: "Music, love and laughter."

*   *   *

E N C O R E

In December, the doctor discovered tumors in the lower intestine, and Mother assented, without complaint, to going into the hospital for surgery. It seemed unlikely she could survive such an assault. Her skin was tissue-paper thin from years of being on cortisone, and both her stamina and spirits had deteriorated since April when her vision had suddenly dimmed and Isabel had died.

The operation lasted over two hours, and Mother not only survived, but the doctor dismissed her within ten days, claiming she was a "tiger." She returned to Hopmeadow, this time to a downstairs room. The room was directly below her old one and identical to it in all respects but one. Instead of a balcony, her doors opened directly onto a little terrace, with lawn and woods beyond.

For several weeks she had meals in her room, or in the day room down the hall. But gradually the urge to return to her friends in the dining room mounted, and she began to stretch her walks each day. She was provided with a wheelchair, which, when she walked behind and pushed, gave her more stable support than the two canes. And when she tired, she could sit down and call for someone to push her.

A P R I L

baby carriage service

As Mother's strength returned, her focus changed from her illness to her surroundings. She knew her next door

neighbor, who was very quiet, woke early in the morning and went out on the terrace for a smoke. Finally she met him, a man, younger by perhaps fifteen years, totally blind. Mother instantly liked his gentlemanliness, and the fact he knew many people she knew.

Daniel, she found, stayed in his room, because he didn't wish to bother people. He ventured only as far as the day room, using his white cane, and counting the paces to find the way back by himself. His meals were brought to his room, where he ate alone.

Mother found that Daniel really enjoyed the sun, as she did, but since their adjoining terrace faced north, he couldn't be in the sun out there. The nurses, he felt, were much too busy to accompany him on a longer stroll. When Mother heard this, she made him a proposition.

"I'm pushing my baby carriage out into the sun. I'll give you a ride. But I'm going to charge 25¢ an hour, which I'll contribute to the solar heated swimming pool."

Daniel graciously accepted, and on every sunny day, when he was not listening to a baseball game, the two of them went out to the sunny, wide walk. Once out there, Dan climbed out of the wheelchair and, holding the right handle, with Mother on the left handle, the two of them strolled along, talking "politics and finance and everything imaginable", interrupted by Mother's occasional commands: "Go right!" or "Go left!" to keep them on the path.

These get-togethers didn't go unnoticed at Hopmeadow, and soon Mother had many requests, which she reported to her family:

"Now the other gentlemen all want rides, so I'm going to charge each of them 25¢ and soon we'll have our pool."

Bob Steele and the bananas

One morning Mother called me at a quarter of seven.

"Are you awake? Do you know what the third largest export of Iceland is?"

I guessed salmon and ice, but neither of these was correct.

"Well, you'll have to think about it, and let me know when you think you've got it," she said. I called her later that day, and she gave me the answer and the story of all the fun she was having with her quiz.

"I listened to Bob Steele yesterday morning on the radio at six, and he said that the third largest export of Iceland is bananas, which are heated by the underground hot springs! I thought that was worth trying out on some others, so I asked everybody I saw if they knew. So far only one nurse guessed right. We had dinner early last night because the board of directors was having a dinner meeting and we had to clear out of the dining room. I saw Daniel Brady before the meeting, and asked him if he knew the third largest export of Iceland, and he didn't, so I told him he could ask the board of directors, and if they couldn't guess the answer, I'd be willing to make a formal appearance!"

"Call me anytime after five in the morning," she offered exuberantly. "I'm awake—and so is Daniel!"

singing our hearts out

Hardly a day went by without a lively report. Here was another day's tale:

"Let me tell you a funny thing. Yesterday I was all British. I put on my kilt and my twin sweater set from Rosemary in London, and I went in and told Daniel what I had on. I went up close to him, so he could feel the big pin

70

on my belt. He said, "We're both British! I'm wearing my Black Watch pants!"

"In the afternoon," she continued, "we had the birthday party for everyone whose birthday falls in April. There was a woman playing the piano, accompanying her daughter, who sang beautifully, and her daughter had a little son. We sang and sang, and sang our hearts out.

"They asked if there were any requests. I said: 'The Sound of Music.' It's the best out of Broadway in years! So they played 'Edelweiss' and someone put the mike right in front of me. I forgot some of the words and just had to sing 'dah, dah, dah. . .' . . I was pretty awful, and much too loud, but it was lots of fun.

"After they were through with that I said, 'Can you play an Aaron Copland number? My granddaughter plays Aaron Copland on the piano and I'd love to hear it again, even though I don't like it!" But the pianist said, 'We're not that good.'

"They were terribly nice people, and I knew they were British, so I said, 'Where in England do you come from?' They said, 'London'. So then I asked, 'What did you do on June 2, twenty-five years ago?' They had to think awhile, and then they said, 'The Coronation!'

"They were there, of course, and I told them I was, too."

a man on my bed

These April days seemed crammed with what Mother labeled 'perfectly harmless fun.' During another pre-breakfast call she reported: "I have been awake since four-thirty. I hear Daniel's door to his terrace open before six. Today I was so wide awake and peppy I decided it would be fun to visit him, but then I decided the nurses would talk too much.

71

"Yesterday was terribly funny. They've been spring-cleaning. Beds, table, pictures, chairs, everything gets taken out of each room and stacked in the corridor. The room gets scrubbed down, and then everything gets put back. Yesterday they did Daniel's room.

"The nurse brought him in to me, using his cane to be sure he didn't bump into things, and he said, 'May I sit on your bed?' There I was, still in my nightgown, flat on my back!"

He sat on the foot of my bed. . . I'll bet that's a first for Hopmeadow! When I had to get up to go to the john, Dan said, 'I'll stand guard at your door.'

"Later that day we went out in the sun. I pushed Daniel, and then we sat on the bench in the sun, and I spread myself like an eagle to get an April tan."

The housekeeper who cleans the rooms each day was particularly fond of both Mother and Daniel, and she carried messages back and forth, assuring them their intrigue would never be divulged by her. Each time she left, she gave Mother a kiss, because Mother reminded her of her own mother.

Always a little concerned about criticism, real or imagined, Mother made this statement in defense of her behavior:

"If my nineteen-year-old grandson from Connecticut, and his seventeen-year-old girlfriend from Michigan, can take their March vacation together unchaperoned, and travel up and down the coast of California all on their own, then I believe (her arthritic finger waving in the air for emphasis) two, grown-up, sensitive, responsible adults should be able to enjoy each other's company and not be criticized—in spite of the difference in our ages!"

the damned denture

Much as she loved service, Mother struggled to take care of herself to the extent that she could. As her vision faded, one task which became more difficult was squeezing the adhesive from the tube onto her denture. She was never quite sure how much was coming out of the tube, or where it was going on the denture. She gave up the task altogether, after she carefully squeezed the tube, eased the denture into place and bit down into a generous mouthful of body lotion.

peanuts and Gary Player

Mother listened to Bob Steele on WTIC every morning, something she had done for possibly forty years. Along with the significant news, Bob tucked in some interesting tidbits that made Mother's day, such as, "Do you know that it's illegal, in Massachusetts, to eat peanuts in church?"

Mother sent word of that along to her minister brother-in-law, Jim, in Oregon.

At nine o'clock every morning she made sure she tuned into Bob reading the names of all the people having eightieth and over birthdays, and sixtieth or over anniversaries. "It's surprising, how many of those people I know," said Mother.

She was thrilled the week the stock market traded 63½ million shares, "the highest week in recorded history of the stock market!"

And she counted the times she heard Gary Player's name mentioned in the course of one day. . . ten, she told everyone. She remembered Gary Player, the golf pro, sitting next to her and Dad, along with Gary's wife, at the pool at the Ocean Club on Paradise Island at Nassau.

"Imagine, the top golfer in the world, making $125,000 in three games. And being considered old, because he's forty-two! Everyone here is thrilled that I knew him. He has that nice South African accent, and he's rather shorter than you'd realize, and I liked his wife very much. How well I remember the spectacular view from the dining hall at the Ocean Club, with some monument off in the distance."

crying jag

Keen as was Mother's sense of joy—or perhaps because her joy was so keen at this moment, other emotions surfaced as well. She reported to me when I went to visit her:

"I started thinking one morning about how good everyone was to me, and I was completely overwhelmed by the goodness about me, and tears began to wallow down my face. I just cried and cried, and the nurses couldn't stop me. I told them, 'I want to cry; these are the first tears in twelve years,' and they were very nice. I finally managed to pull myself together and got to the dining room for lunch. After lunch I went to Mildred's room, because I had something to tell her, but she wasn't there, so I left a message with the nurse to tell her to come to my room.

"When she arrived, I said, 'Mildred, I'm glad I didn't die!' Mil said, 'What on earth are you talking about?'

"So I told her about the time two and a half years ago, just before I came here, when my whole face hurt so much. My dentist was away, so I called another dentist, and he came and took out four teeth. I was in such pain, I said, 'I cannot take it anymore.' I decided I'd had a long, full life, and nobody would miss me.

74

"I sat on the edge of my bed, and counted out twelve pills and said, 'that ought to do it, come heaven or hell.'

"Next morning Payson found me, and couldn't wake me, so he called the ambulance, and I was taken to the hospital, where they revived me.

"But now I've been here over two years, and I'm really glad I didn't die, and I just wanted you to know, and I'm going to tell my children, too, because I've never told anyone, and it's been a secret for the past two years."

She offered Mildred a half a cup of wine, and the nurse brought them each a serving. Mildred polished hers off very quickly. Mother said, "I'm not going to give you any more. I consider you've had quite enough."

Later, Mother told me she thought that with a new set of teeth, hips and eyes, she'd be as good as new and perhaps last until she was one hundred.

"I'm not senile. I'm terribly aware of what's going on," she declared. "I just hope I never become like some of these people here, with their poor, burned-out brains. I'm so lucky. Some people have to be tied into their chairs, and don't have any minds. Don't ever do that to me. Get me out of the way as fast as possible. I've been thinking a lot about euthanasia recently, and I think it's a good idea."

the squeaky voice

My husband and I were in Philadelphia, visiting his mother, when an early morning call came from Mother.

"I tracked you down," she explained, hoarse and breathless. "I just wanted you to hear my strange voice! It's too funny for words."

She'd had a cold, and a cough, and had ventured out to go swimming at a nearby school's indoor pool early one evening. The cold subsided, but the hoarseness persisted and turned into a squeaky voice. Dr. Harmon suggested to her she stop talking, but Mother told him, "I can't stop talking. If I stop, nobody says anything. There are just too many things of interest. I've *got* to talk."

However, she did try to comply with the doctor's advice, so when he left her room, she went next door to Daniel's room to collect him for their walk, and she leaned over very close to him so she could whisper in his ear. Not knowing she was that close, Daniel moved, and his hip collided with her forehead. According to Mother, "I was almost knocked over, so I had to turn around and lie on his bed! After I'd got my circulation going again, I took Daniel in my buggy, and we went outside and sat in the sun for an hour. It was lovely. The sun was the highest it's been."

A specialist came to check the misbehaving throat, and she told him: "Before you inspect me, I want you to know I've been thinking way back, and if I'm peculiar, it's perhaps because I played the cornet when I was very young. I was told I would develop very strong lungs."

The doctor checked her out and then said he'd like to have x-rays done at the hospital. "But we have a machine for that right here," Mother said.

"You do?," he asked.

"Yes," Mother replied to the young doctor. "You may have to retire someday yourself. You should know all about this place!"

The specialist found she had a partially paralyzed vocal chord, and Mother concluded it was from singing too loudly at the cocktail party.

"If I go, Dr. Harmon goes. . ."

Mother felt quite frisky, in spite of her voice and the extra exertion it took to make her words understood. She found herself using spicy language she hardly expected at times. "I wonder," she said, "where I got this awful vocabulary! Words just seem to come out!" She warned Dr. Harmon:

"If the Board of Directors decides I'm too frisky, and I have to leave Hopmeadow, then you'll have to go too, because it's you who's given me all these pills that make me behave this way. We'll go together, with a rum drink between us!"

the parsley package

During the cold and coughing stage Mother stayed in bed, and her meals were brought to her on a tray. She missed being at her table, so she decided to stir up a little fun. "I found I had parsley on my supper tray, one evening. Lindy loves parsley. I can't eat it. I don't like it, but when I'm at the table, Lindy makes me eat it. He says it's good for me. So I took my parsley, and made a little package, wrapping it up very carefully, and I called in the young male aid, and asked him: "Can you spare five minutes? Would you please take this to Lindy in the dining room, and tell him I sent it with motherly love! And wait and see what he says."

Word came back that the whole table loved it, and everyone had quite a laugh over the parsley package.

mind over matter

In the middle of the night, one night, Mother summoned the nurse to ask for some throat lozenges to suck on to make her sore throat feel better. The nurse tucked one under Mother's tongue and left some spares on her bedside table where Mother could reach them easily when she woke up.

"I went off to sleep for two hours," she reported, "and then I woke up again and reached out and found one and put it under my tongue. It felt awfully good, and I went right off to sleep again. When I woke up in the morning, it was still under my tongue, and the nurse found it still had the wrapping on! So it was mind over matter!"

the wrong Daniel

Fanny stopped by for a visit one day, while Mom was confined to her bed. As she left, Mother asked Fanny to drop in and see Daniel, since Daniel didn't see many people in a day. Fanny, now Chairman of the Council, thought Mother meant Daniel Brady, the Director of Hopmeadow, instead of her next-door neighbor, so she stopped by the Director's office and reported: "Laura Hunter asked me to stop by and see you, since you don't see many people in a day." When the error was discovered, everyone roared with laughter.

M A Y

diary on display

I had typed up Mother's original diary and put it in a binder and left it in her bookcase. Although she could no longer see to read it, Mother decided the time had come to share it, and that Hannah should be the first to do so, as she was one of the first to be mentioned in it. So Mother took it up to her room, but Hannah wasn't there, so she left it.

"I knew I'd hear from her eventually," Mom said, who was still taking meals in her room.

"Sure enough, a few days later Hannah arrived, walking along slowly with her walker. She was all enthusiasm. She said she lost sleep over it, and she couldn't put it down, and had stitches over parts of it.

"We had a lovely visit. I told her I used to be scared pink of her, and didn't dare open my trap, and she said, 'We know each other better now.'

"Hannah commented on the diary: 'You do seem to be drinking a lot.' I told her, 'My mother was a member of the Women's Christian Temperance Association and I *never* had a drink until after I was married.' I hope that doesn't make my husband sound too bad!"

head to head with Daniel

Mother told me one day that she might be moving from her present room to a room on the other side of Daniel's room.

"Daniel very thoughtfully suggested that I might prefer that room over the one I'm in because it's carpeted, and mine is not. It's like a hospital. The other room is being vacated by a quadraplegic who is planning to go home in July. And," she added, "Daniel and I would be closer—our doors would be right next to each other."

I agreed with her that their doors would be closer, but mentioned that with the present arrangement, their beds were backed up against the same wall, so that their *heads* were actually very close together.

Later Mother reported to me she'd had the courage to tell Daniel what I'd said, and he said, "I've been thinking the very same thing! Our heads are just *inches* apart!"

Daniel's daughter was married in May, and Mother checked Dan just before he left for the wedding, to see that he was dressed properly.

"You're not going to wear your golf cap, are you?" she asked. He showed her the handkerchief in his breast pocket, and Mother told him, "Tell your family that you're a great inspiration to me and to all of us here at Hopmeadow. You're the nicest gentleman here, and we're all proud of you."

That night at 8:15, when Mother was getting ready for bed, she told the nurse, "Give me my bathrobe! I want to see how Daniel fared at the wedding." She went in and found him fast asleep.

Next morning she went in again, and said, "You were asleep at 8:15. You must have had too much to drink."

"I admit it," Daniel said. "I had champagne and cocktails. I didn't realize I fell asleep so early."

Daniel had a ball game to listen to, so that afternoon Mother went out alone with her 'baby carriage' and sat in the sun.

a great inspiration

Mother had a "great inspiration" one morning at ten o'clock. "I decided to call my sister in Oregon."

Unable to look up the number in the book, she simply dialed the operator, and said, "I don't have the number, or the street, I just have the name, and the town, Corvallis, Oregon.

"By gosh," she reported, "in two minutes, Jim (the Congregational minister) came on the phone, sounding very sleepy. It was seven o'clock there. I said I wanted to speak to Florence. She was so amazed at my squeaky voice, it took some getting used to. I told her I wanted to correct a statement of my younger sister, that I had a new boyfriend.

"I want you to know he's sixty-eight. He's a friend, not a boyfriend.

"Florence said Jim had a message: 'He wants to be sure he can officiate at your wedding, if there's a wedding.'

"I replied, 'I've already engaged him to take care of my funeral, not my wedding.'"

Later, my husband and I visited Mother, close to her

80

eighty-third birthday on May 29, and she told us, somewhat coquettishly: "I've decided I'm going to stay sixty!"

"Does this have something to do with Daniel?," I asked.

"He's sixty-eight," she admitted, and a sentimental tear rolled down her cheek. "He has shown me more respect than any man in the past twelve and a half years."

For her "sixtieth" birthday, Mother had a fresh permanent wave. As she was wheeled in her chair down the hallway afterwards, Mother reported, "everyone said I looked gorgeous. I felt like the Queen herself. I kept bowing my head and waving my hand. We had a laugh! Then I dressed up in my blue and white embroidered dress from Madeira. Everybody loved it."

Mother attended one more Assembly meeting, and reported that when it came to new business, "nobody said one damn word. So I stood up, and in my croaky voice, I said, 'Can you hear me, Mr. Chairman? Where does the greenhouse fund stand now? When it's finished, it's time to start on the swimming pool fund.'"

J U N E

the little engine that could

An invitation came to attend her granddaughter's graduation nearby, and Mother said, "By golly, if I feel well enough, I'm going to go. Eliza is graduating *cum laude*. Not only is she beautiful, but she's smart as well. I do seem to have smart grandchildren. I often ask, 'I wonder whose fault it is?' Even if I don't feel well, I'm going to go by just saying to myself, like the 'Little Engine That Could', 'I think I can, I think I can.'"

She made it, and reported:

"The ceremony was held out-of-doors, in the shade under the trees. Ben got there early, and reserved front row seats. They wheeled my chair right plunk in the center; I sat between Ben and Kati. Right in front of us were all the faculty in caps and gowns. The girls came in, two by two, all in long, white gowns. Organ music was piped in. The graduation speaker was a Senator from Missouri, with a great, big voice and a good sense of humor. Eliza was given two prizes. When it was over I found, of all people, Dr. Harmon. One of his daughters was in the graduating class, too. I said to him, 'It was so beautiful, I've been crying for an hour.' He said, 'Don't worry, everyone else has, too.' It was comforting to hear that from my doctor.

"Andy brought me back home. I was in no condition to go into the dining room, so I went back to my room, where they brought me my lunch on a tray."

Seabrook supporter

The second large nuclear protest at Seabrook, New Hampshire took place with grandson Paul participating actively. The week before the 1978 Occupation/Restoration, Paul rode his bike with a group called "the Solar Rollers" across Massachusetts from Amherst, into southern New Hampshire, stopping along the way to alert people to the dangers of nuclear power. Now quite sympathetic, Mother listened to news on the radio, hoping she'd hear his name. A few days after the peaceful demonstration, the Nuclear Regulatory Commission called a temporary halt to construction. Mother telephoned early in the morning when she heard that on the radio, and croaked out triumphantly, "Paul Memhard has won!"

"Edelweiss"

Mother's appetite subsided, and some days she felt quite nauseous. The doctor order a liver scan, and then gave the news to Ben.

"Your mother has cancer in the liver, and other places as well. She doesn't have long to live."

Ben told the news to Mother. "How long?", she asked. "Three years?" "No, Mom. They don't know, but they think three weeks to three months."

She and Ben had a big, "beautiful" cry together.

I spent the next day with her, and Mother had decided that everyone might as well know, so she told Fanny to tell her table mates, each privately, so as not to spoil their meal. Then she decided to write letters. She'd recently received one from her granddaughter, Laura, still at school in California, now getting her certification in massage. Mother dictated:

Dear Laura,

I was delighted to have your lovely letter. I am dictating to your nice mother, who is spending a lovely, long day with me while your father goes off to New Hampshire on business.

I honestly thought that you were crazy to go off into the massage business which I thought the Swedes had a monopoly on. But your letter, in detail, demonstrates you aren't so crazy! It's turned out to be a great new interest and certainly a new one to me.

You will dislike having to know that my time on this earth is limited. To how many weeks or months they cannot now tell. They have discovered I have cancer in my liver and various other places. I can't imagine what it will be like not to be alive and having fun, particularly with my family, of all of whom I have been very proud.

I hope you won't shed too many tears over this news, but will have a good laugh over the many funny things that have happened during our lives. I have had eighty-three memorable years.

You may not hear from me again, but I love you dearly. And I'm sure you can look forward to a very happy life.

Love and kisses,

Granny

Then she remembered Laura had just celebrated her twenty-first birthday, so she enclosed a check for $21.

Next, Mother wanted to discuss arrangements for her service.

"I don't want a funeral," she declared emphatically. "I just want a simple, memorial service by the grave, with just close family there. And if my brother-in-law, Jim, can't make it, because he's so far away, then I would like to have Brenda do the service. She's Mildred's minister, and she's very young and attractive. I remember, when she visited here, she sat on the end of the bed, with her legs dangling, and she was great fun. She appeals to me. I don't think it matters, do you, what church it is? It doesn't matter to me. I like Brenda, and I think you children would all enjoy her, too."

So we placed a call to Brenda and arranged for her to visit the following day. "If you sing at the service, said Mom, "sing 'Edelweiss'. I like that 'specially, because I saw it growing in the Austrian Alps. And I like 'Climb Every Mountain,' too, but that would be hard.

"One more thing, Polly," Mom said.

"I don't want to suffer. If I'm suffering, and I can't take it anymore, I want a little pill. But I'm going to tell the doctor, it *has* to be green, because my favorite color is green."

The nurse brought Mother her evening pills and laxative. Mother downed the pills and took most of the laxative, handing the cup back to the nurse.

"Here, you can have the rest," she said.

"And I want you to tell the Chairman of the Board, I've had a b.m."

don't be beguiled

Mildred appeared for her evening visit. She wheeled her chair in, under her own power, all the way up alongside the bed as close as she could get to Mother, and the two of them clasped hands as they do every night.   ·

"I'm glad to see you," Mother said.

"You're not home very much," said Mil. "I think you spend too much time next door."

"I do not. But Polly took Daniel and me out for a nice walk today, and she took our picture. What have you been doing? I want a report."

"Well, I had a kiss from a man today."

"Who was it?"

"I don't have to tell you."

"You'd better," said Mom. "You can't keep any secrets from me."

"It was a relative of yours. A very nice man."

"My son, Ben, I'll bet. But he wasn't here today. It was yesterday."

"I think it was Ben. Anyway, it was a nice, big buss, right here," pointing, "on the cheek." She turned to me and said, "I'm losing my wits, you know. I don't remember too well, and sometimes I have trouble formulating words."

Mom said, "You know, it's because of you and Ben that I'm here, don't you? When I was in the hospital, and Ben was looking around at different places, he came here, and you were almost the first person he saw, and he said, 'If it's good enough for Mildred, it's good enough for my mother.'

She then pulled Mildred close. "I have something to tell you, and I don't want you to be sad. The doctor has told my family that I have cancer in my liver and I don't have very long to live."

Mildred calmly replied, "You shouldn't believe that doctor."

"Why? I like him," Mother said. "He proved to me he has a heart. I always thought he didn't give a damn. But yesterday he couldn't tell me, he told my son, Ben, and Ben told me."

"Well, don't believe him. And don't be beguiled by him. I've had cancer eight times, and I'm still here. I've never worried about it."

"Well, they cut yours out and it was gone. They can't cut mine out, because I've only got one liver."

"How old are you?", Mildred asked.

"Eighty-three."

"Well, I'll keep a sharp eye on you, and if I catch you worrying, you'll be in trouble. I like you."

"I think that's funny!" said Mother, giggling.

"What's funny about that?" protested Mildred. "You rascal. . ." she said fondly, patting Mother's hand.

"Well, I'm going now, and leave you two to your visit. But I'll be around to be sure you're not worrying."

And they gave each other a big, goodnight hug.

a last request

During my last visit with Mother she was drowsy but not in pain. She had ceased to eat, and could no longer speak. The nurses turned her frequently, and they spoke to her lovingly. Roused, she smiled broadly when she heard my voice, and began to wave her hand in the air, spelling words with her finger. I couldn't understand, so I put a pen in her hand and held her journal close. Slowly she spelled out the words on a large, blank page: "Letter from Laura."

A letter was sitting on her bedside table, and she wanted to be sure I had read it. I opened the envelope and read aloud:

Dear Granny,

I am in Colorado, spending a month studying *en route* home. Right now I'm sitting outside the Boulder library in a wet shirt, having just tubed down the Boulder Creek, water cold and fast. Last week I climbed in the Rocky Mountains, moving in barefoot ecstasy through swamps and over snow.

I received your letter just as I was getting ready to leave Palo Alto. I was very sad to hear that your body has taken on the cancer. Such news brings the passage of days new awareness.

You were with me in the mountains as I laughed and wondered at the purple columbine, the yellow cactus flowers, and the little, white blossoms hiding amongst the rocks at the very top of the Divide.

I love you very much. Till August.

Laura

Mother died on August seventh. On August ninth, Brenda conducted the service, and the family and close friends gathered by the graveside and sang, as best we could:

"Edelweiss, Edelweiss,
Bless my homeland forever."

E P I L O G U E

As the journal was prepared for publication and read by many people, a number of questions were raised. What was Laura's medical history? What about those drugs—what were they, and to what extent did they help, or hinder her health? What insights can the professionals who treated her at Hopmeadow Home give us about Laura? Was she typical of an aging woman; in what ways was she unusual?

Perhaps even more importantly, what can *we* do to ensure health, vitality and productive activity for the rest of *our* lives? Is disease a necessary companion of old age, or can we undertake a life style, food, exercise and health care that will enable us to live in good health to the fullness of our years?

To suggest some answers, I have included a medical history of Laura while in Hopmeadow Home, based on interviews and excerpts from medical records, and a chapter by Ken Dychtwald, a leading gerontologist. His work, along with that of many others involved in holistic and macrobiotic approaches to health and nutrition, reinforces my heartfelt conviction, based on Mother's example, that the older years can be the most creative; that the resources of older people are boundless; and that new ways of living together in dignity, independence and health need to be examined and established.

Polly Memhard
Riverside, CT, October, 1981

FROM HOPMEADOW
REPORTS & INTERVIEWS

On her entry, the Hopmeadow doctor described Laura as "infirm, querulous, slightly agitated." She had osteoarthritis, with fusion in both hips; she was ambulatory with two canes. She had glaucoma. She had a dental problem with recent removal of teeth from loss of supporting jawbone and experienced discomfort with her lower denture. She had "tardive dyskinesia" which is smacking of lips and tongue and she also rubbed her feet constantly. Both actions are side effects of certain drugs, especially Valium. She complained of constipation, dizziness, insomnia and shortness of breath. She lost twelve pounds following her entry into the home. Her medication at the home initially consisted of Elavil, Valium, Tylenol, Dramamine, Mylanta and Motrin.

A staff member noted: "Laura was not looking forward to coming to Hopmeadow Home. There is always an adjustment period, which is much easier if someone is looking forward to being here. Laura was not thrilled with the prospect, but was accepting. She needed time to adjust, to see what was going on and relax. We set the stage for her response. We weren't sure how much potential she had, whether she could manage the rest home unit which had less care than the nursing unit, which would require her to walk to the dining room three times a day. We had to be a bit tough, a little rough on her, and it wasn't easy."

"Initially she was very despondent", said one nurse. "At first she used her teeth as an excuse not to chat. It's sometimes difficult to know how much physical discomfort a person has, and how much is depression."

"Fortunately she knew some people from before, like Millie, who told the staff what she had been like. And she had a supportive family. This is very important. It helps a great deal if there are frequent visits and phone calls and loving care."

"She was not interested in reading or watching t.v., saying 'I want to save my eyes.' She went to the dining room, but rushed through her meals eating little and rushed back to her room. She lay on her bed with her feet elevated, and when asked to participate in an activity, she replied 'I'm too ill.' Her denture didn't fit comfortably and she was embarrassed about her appearance and poor diction."

In November, a psychiatrist prescribed the drug Stelazine. "That opened the door, and we followed through and wouldn't let her close it again," said a nurse. "We insisted she come out of her room for a drink, and she did, explaining to people she was 'following doctor's orders.' We braced ourselves, expecting her to be uncooperative, but figured with patience she would respond. The recreational therapist presented her with a choice of three activities. Pretty soon she perked up, to such an extent that it seemed like the Stelazine was a miracle drug, and we thought we'd try it on others as well, but unfortunately, it didn't have the same effect on anyone else! This made us think, all the more, that she was on the verge of coming out anyway. How much would have happened without the drug, we don't really know, and won't ever know."

The staff noted she turned off her radio during a visit from family, and began to go outside by herself and attend reading groups. She showed more interest in her appearance and began to go to the hairdresser. She even left the home for a two day visit with family.

By May, the doctor noted, she was "less depressed, happy, in fact." Her high point was election as a Unit Representative, a job with recognition and responsibility. In October, the doctor noted "improved attitude—euphoric."

Her medication, which was reviewed once a month, at this point included Stelazine, Unicap vitamins, Dramamine, Milk of Magnesia, Dalmane, Tylenol and an occasional douche and Fleets enema, with Hydrodiuril when elevated blood pressure was noted. The tardive dyskinesia was gone.

The nurses now thoroughly enjoyed her and felt she was giving them a good deal in return for their care. "To see someone come alive as she did was really heartwarming. From someone who wouldn't speak, to someone who would call you in, was remarkable. I can't remember anyone else we've had such a change in. She was an exciting person, she was precious," said a nurse. "She was a lady—a lady-lady. She would say to me, 'I'm glad I went all the places I did. If you ever get a chance to go places, —go!'"

In June, she fell, her vision dimmed very quickly, and her good friend Isabel died. Nurses reported, "Conversations lapsed into brief words, said with effort." Offered talking books, Laura replied that she was unable to concentrate. A psychiatrist found "no signs of organic deficit", noted her regression, found her uninterested in talking about the death of her friend, about whom she simply said, "I knew she was going to die." He increased the anti-depressant and recommended a program of resocialization.

In December, following symptoms of anorexia (loss of appetite), hypochronic, macrocytic anemia and blood in the stool, she was hospitalized and a surgeon removed two primary carcinomas from the sigmoid colon and right colon, with no evidence of metastases.

In May, she was active again, had made good friends

with her blind neighbor, and even went swimming. She had a cold with hoarseness which persisted and was accompanied by anorexia and weakness. A liver scan showed metastatic disease. She was given 15 mg. daily of Prednisone, changed to 10 mgs. every other day with some improvement of her symptomology. However, the doctor noted, she went "relentlessly downhill with increasing weakness, lethargy, anorexia, poor oral intake and ultimately . . . death" on 8/7/78.

"She didn't let anything get her down," said a nurse. "She took minimal medicine, and put up with being turned and having a lamp for her sore hips, and she always tried to have a smile. She loved to be touched, but she wasn't clingy. She's the only patient I knew who died with real dignity. She was prepared to die, mentally, physically and spiritually. She went through what is called the 'life integration' process. Not too many do this, —she was one of the rare ones here who did it. But if you've had a satisfying life, and you have family and people who care for you, you don't just look at the present, you fit it in to your whole life. She said, 'I've had a long life, it's time for others now.' She died peacefully. She made us all very happy. Someone like her makes our work worthwhile."

THE REST OF *OUR* LIVES:
A POSITIVE APPROACH TO AGING

by Ken Dychtwald, Ph.D.

Creative Aging

Laura Hunter has done combat with some of the negative images of aging in her unique journal. She has given us a new model and upset the usual stereotype of the nursing home resident. Spunky, resourceful, and surprising to herself as well as to family, friends and the staff of Hopmeadow Home, she has demonstrated that the time spent in a nursing home need not be dismal, but can be a time of personal growth and fulfillment.

In traditional, pre-industrial societies, elders were loved and revered and served as active participants in family and community events and decisions. Our recent youth-oriented culture has disrupted such patterns, through later marriages and children growing up too late to know their grandparents; through young people moving away from home to attend college, get married, strike out on their own—and then disengaging themselves from active involvement in the lives of their parents and grandparents. Additionally, many elders choose to live in retirement communities, while younger and middle aged people often select "age ghettos" in which to live. Mandatory retirement excludes older people from the work force, at the same time that youth-focused city "planning" has often created environments which are scarcely navigable and often dangerous for elders, and which negate, instead of support, inter-generational contact. Sadly, the "ageist" messages from such conditions, instead of causing outrage, are all too often internalized by older people into attitudes of resignation, sickness, and low self-esteem, which further translate into frustration, tension, unhappiness, loneliness, stress, and even perhaps a lessening of the will to live.

Whereas disease and death in America used to result primarily from natural disasters, infant mortality and infectious diseases, the second half of the twentieth century has shown a dramatic rise in the incidence of stress-related disorders. The primary killers and cripplers are now cardiovascular and respiratory diseases, cancer and arthritis, which are all "lifestyle-related" disorders.

What this suggests is that we have done very poorly at initiating and maintaining the kinds of healthy lifestyles, nutritional habits and exercise activities that would fortify us against the often debilitating and stressful influence of modern living. We cannot blame germs or doctors, when so many people shy away from taking responsibility for nutritional habits, meaningful social and political involvement, stimulating intellectual activities, and vitalizing body movements and exercise.

On the positive side, there is a growing national trend toward health promotion, personal growth and self-improvement, and it is beginning to filter into the world of the elderly.

At present, however, most counseling and medical services for the elderly are *not* focused on eliciting health, joy and creativity, but instead deal primarily with problem-oriented treatment, therapy, chemical prescription, and pass-time activities. This form of clinical approach does little to enrich and fortify the lives of the elderly and thereby encourage the development of overall health, responsibility and well-being, nor does it effectively lessen the negative and deteriorating influence of stressful and unfulfilling lifestyles. Many critics of contemporary health care go so far as to suggest that our health-care systems are "iatrogenic"— that they seem to be creating more disease, through insensitive care, reckless drug use, and reductionistic methods, than they are eliminating. For example, the emphasis on symptom-treating therapy seems to have created a monster in the form of prescribed drug abuse, as the quantity of drugs consumed by Americans has already increased one hundredfold during this present century.

Holistic Approaches to Health & Aging

Without denying the importance of the more traditional approaches in appropriate situations, numerous new programs are beginning to find that vitalizing and stress-reducing exercise, interesting and meaningful social-interaction programs, nutritional guidance and inter-generational activities can go a long way toward enriching the lives of older adults while simultaneously improving health, well-being and self-esteem.

Although this new approach is still in its embryonic stage, it is based on the underlying belief that aging can be experienced as a full and thoroughly rewarding growth and maturation process and that the later years of life can hold within them a unique freedom to learn, explore, and share. Inherent in this "holistic" approach to health care is a deep appreciation for the unity of mind, body, and spirit, a strong emphasis on preventative education and self responsibility, and the belief that growth, exercise, good nutrition and meaningful interpersonal involvement are necessary ingredients in the healthy life-style.

In recent years, many alternatives to traditional counseling and medicine have emerged. Techniques such as biofeedback, autogenics, relaxation and stress-reduction training, yoga, meditation, art and dance therapy, t'ai chi, and various types of "growth" groups for elders have been met with strong and positive response from elders and health practitioners nationwide who prefer preventative and holistic approaches to health. Reflecting the need for treating the "whole person," there has also been a re-emergence of interest in health-team oriented clinics wherein various types of physical and mental health professionals and lay professionals effectively share and blend skills and resources.

Older people using these approaches have undergone some remarkable transformations: minds and memories become refreshed and alert; many diagnosed as senile turn out to be merely lonely and bored; and a lot of people who are supposed to be hard of hearing discover they are really just alienated; it's been a long time since they've been able to talk to someone in a meaningful way. Relaxation techniques allow people to sleep better and feel refreshed without drugs. Through exercises, people rebuild muscles that improve walking, breathing and posture. On a healthy, nutritious diet, people find their bodies lighter, cleaner, more alive and vigorous. With muscles toned and blood flowing, people become less sick, more involved in each other's lives on satisfying and stimulating levels.

Laura Hunter's journal indicates she was very well cared for, in an exceptionally fine nursing home. But it took unusual determination on her part to maintain the positive spirit which she did. She was not aware of the growing conspiracy which exists today to change the images and the activities of elderly people and nursing home residents. Were she alive today, I would have liked to introduce her to other members of this courageous conspiracy. But for benefit of the reader, examples are listed below of successful new programs that represent the kind of social concern, clinical sensitivity and program ingenuity that are helping to create the possibility of healthier and happier futures for all of us.

Model programs for the elderly

Seniors Health Program, Augustana Hospital, 411 West Dickens Avenue, Chicago, IL 60614. Created in 1975 to provide older people with helpful information about medications, their uses and effects, and to sensitize medical professionals to the emotional and physical needs of the elderly. Programs include training materials, workshops, lectures, and a variety of helpful senior health manuals.

Senior Health Source (SHS), 1024 Washington Street, Albuquerque, N.M., 87108. Created in 1975 as an informal "health club" for elders, now expanded to twenty locations, including housing sites, meal sites, a senior citizen's center and a Senior Day Care Center.

Senior Actualization and Growth Explorations (SAGE), 114 Montecito Avenue, Oakland, CA 94610. Started in 1974 to generate positive images of aging. Staffed by twenty psychologists, physicians, breathing, movement and art therapists, SAGE has extended its resources into nursing homes, community centers, hospitals, universities, medical centers, growth centers and health clinics. SAGE staff have trained more than twenty thousand health professionals in their "holistic" approach throughout the United States.

Elvirita Lewis Foundation, 230 Third Avenue, Santa Cruz, CA 95062, has organized free dental clinics, made possible the distribution of free produce to elders, published a Resource Directory for Elders for the Santa Cruz area, and fulfilled their motto of "elders serving others" through a Senior Companion Program and an Intergenerational Child Care Center.

Nursing Home Residents Advisory Council (NHRAC), 111 East Franklin, Suite 210, Minneapolis, MN 55404. Run by and for nursing home and boarding care home residents in Minnesota. Membership exceeds four thousand, effectively demonstrating that the institutionalized elderly respond positively to opportunities for self-improvement and self-governance.

The Bridge Project, Fairhaven College, Bellingham, WA 98225. The nation's first attempt to bring older people completely into college life, through attending classes and receiving credits and degrees along with regular students while living in a remodeled dormitory and participating in college events.

Elderhostel, 100 Boylston Street, Suite 200R, Boston, MA 02116. Combines the traditions of education and hosteling, for elder citizens on the move. A network of over 300 colleges and universities in 50 states and Canada which offers special, low-cost, one-week residential academic programs for older adults, mostly during the summer but some in other seasons as well, open to people over sixty or to those whose spouse qualifies. Many hostelers attend several courses throughout the country, making new friends, expanding their horizons and traveling and living in comfortable, secure and minimally-priced settings.

The Gray Panthers, 3700 Chestnut Street, Philadelphia, PA 19104, is a national coalition of old, young,and middle-aged activists that has become an outspoken national movement. This group of "radical elders," numbering more than ten thousand, is committed to the creation of a society in which self-actualization, health, and human values receive the highest priority.

Ken Dychtwald, Ph.D., psychologist, is a pioneer in the holistic health and human development fields. He is founding president of the Association for Humanistic Gerontology (AHG), and was formerly the director of the SAGE project. His publications include BODYMIND (1977); with Albert Villoldo, MILLENIUM: GLIMPSES INTO THE 21st CENTURY (1981), and numerous articles in professional journals and popular magazines.

Laura, Circa 1948

Polly, 1980

For additional copies of THE REST OF MY LIFE, contact your local bookstore or write:

Growing Pains Press, 22 Fifth Street, Suite 204
Stamford, CT 06905 (203) 348-6860